D0881162

José Lezama Lima's Joyful Vision

The Texas Pan American Series

José Lezama Lima's Joyful Vision

· · · · · · · · · · ·

A Study of *Paradiso* and Other Prose Works

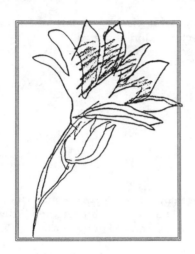

by
Gustavo Pellón

University of Texas Press   Austin

First edition, 1989

Requests for permission to reproduce material from this work should
be sent to Permissions, University of Texas Press, Box 7819, Austin,
TX 78713-7819.

Library of Congress Cataloging-in-Publication Data

Pellón, Gustavo.
    José Lezama Lima's joyful vision : a study of Paradiso and other
prose works / by Gustavo Pellón. — 1st ed.
      p.   cm.—(The Texas Pan American series)
    Bibliography: p.
    Includes index.
    ISBN 0-292-74020-4 (alk. paper)
    1. Lezama Lima, José—Prose. 2. Lezama Lima, José. Paradiso.
I. Title. II. Series.
PQ7389.L49Z83   1989
868—dc20   89-4856
                                                          CIP

The paper used in this publication meets the minimum requirements
of American National Standard for Information Sciences—Perma-
nence of Paper for Printed Library Materials, ANSI Z39.48-1984. ⊚

The Texas Pan American Series is published with the assistance of a
revolving publication fund established by the Pan American Sulphur
Company.

Excerpts from the works of José Lezama Lima reprinted by permission
of Eloísa Lezama Lima and Agencia Literaria Latinoamericana.

Excerpts from PARADISO by José Lezama Lima, translated by
Gregory Rabassa. Translation copyright © 1974 by Farrar, Straus and
Giroux. Reprinted by permission of Farrar, Straus and Giroux, Inc.

Some material in Chapter 2 previously appeared in *Hispamérica*;
earlier versions of Chapters 3 and 6 appeared in *Revista de Estudios
Hispánicos* and *Modern Language Notes* respectively. Reprinted by
permission of Ediciones Hispamérica, Vassar College, and Johns
Hopkins University Press, respectively.

For Karen, Nicolás, and Sofía

Contents

Illustrations

Preface

MY PURPOSE IN writing this book has not been to provide an introduction to the work of José Lezama Lima. Such introductory works have been available now for some years. I believe that the criticism on Lezama has reached a point where we can begin to examine his works in the context not only of Hispanic literature but of world literature and current literary theory.

Although Lezama's production as a poet was vast and important, he himself repeatedly stated that the novel *Paradiso* was the *summa* of his poetry. Taking up his paradoxical challenge, I have chosen to study his poetics primarily through his acknowledged prose masterpiece. The extra-generic terrain of this poem-novel is to my mind the best place to illustrate Lezama's poetic brinksmanship. Concentrating on his major prose works—*Paradiso, Oppiano Licario*, and his essays—I have sought to explain Lezama's theory and practice of literature. Throughout the book I have been fascinated by the stimulating difficulties that Lezama's work presents. I have sought to highlight and preserve rather than resolve the essential and persistent contradictions in his writings: the mystical quest for illumination through obscurity, his calculated cultivation of naïveté, his cosmopolitan Americanism, his Proust-like fascination with and ultimate condemnation of homosexuality, his modernist (in some aspects even postmodernist) narrative style coupled with a mystical (and essentially medieval) worldview. Above all, I have wanted to share my wonder at Lezama, true "monstruo de su laberinto," who in an age of pessimism maintained his joyful vision.

Acknowledgments

TO JOHN INCLEDON, who first spoke to me about Lezama and invited me to read my first paper about him, I register my gratitude. Julio Rodríguez-Luis does not share my enthusiasm for Lezama, but the generous and friendly dialogue we have maintained since I wrote a graduate seminar paper with him has helped me refine my position. I wish Emir Rodríguez Monegal could see that the paper he read and received with enthusiasm has now grown to be a book; his encouragement was decisive. Many people received my evolving work on Lezama with warmth: Saúl Sosnowski, Sara Castro-Klarén, Francisco J. Cevallos, David T. Gies, Javier Herrero, Enrico Mario Santí, Randolph Pope, Eugenio Suárez-Galbán, Gustavo Pérez Firmat, and René Prieto. I thank them all for their support along the way.

Roberto González Echevarría, Donald L. Shaw, and Tobin Siebers read the manuscript with great care, pointed out infelicities, and offered valuable suggestions. Roger Shattuck read Chapter 6 and gave useful advice. Gail Moore and the staff of the University of Virginia's College of Arts and Sciences' Word Processing Center taught me to use a word processor and printed many drafts. I owe a special word of thanks to my friend Richard Vassos, whose generous offer of support gave me much peace of mind.

I would also like to thank the various publishers and institutions that gave me permission to reproduce illustrations and previously published material. They are identified on the copyright page and in the illustration captions.

The final word I reserve for Karen Resnick Pellón, my wife, without whom this book simply would not have been written. Thanks.

A Note on Translations

WHENEVER POSSIBLE I have used Gregory Rabassa's translation of *Paradiso* (Austin: University of Texas Press, 1988). In those cases where my analysis required a more literal rendering, I have done the translation myself. In other cases I have ventured to bring Rabassa's translation closer to the original. All departures from Rabassa's translation are enclosed in brackets. Unless otherwise noted, all other translations are mine. All references to Lezama's works are to the Aguilar edition of the *Obras Completas* in two volumes and are given in parentheses in the text.

Chapter 1

Introduction: Beyond the Aesthetics of Realism

Genre is reborn and renewed at every new stage in the development of literature and in every individual work of a given genre. This constitutes the life of the genre.
—Mikhail Bakhtin, Problems of Dostoevsky's Poetics

If there is any difficulty in classifying this book as a novel it is because that form has been generally considered from a perspective imposed by realism.
—Emir Rodríguez Monegal,
"Paradiso: Una silogística del sobresalto"

• • •

José Lezama Lima's novel *Paradiso* has provoked widely different reactions from critics since its publication in 1966. Attempts have been made to read the novel within the tradition of realist aesthetics, a Bakhtinian reading has been proposed that challenges the pertinence of that realist evaluation, and finally a poststructuralist reading, advanced principally by the novelist Severo Sarduy, has developed certain insights of the Bakhtinian reading in order to make far-reaching ideological claims. While these three critical approaches have each contributed to our understanding of a work that has proved particularly resistant to classification, they seem to make either too little or too much of what *Paradiso* actually offers. The reading I will set forth builds on a dialogue with these critical contributions, but seeks to preserve a difficult and delicate balance that I consider to be Lezama's major contribution to the genre of fiction.

Lezama's aesthetics place the highest value on the production of a stream of images and analogies that flow from each other by association, pushing the readers to the limits of their interpretive faculties. The privileged role he accords to imagery necessarily leads Lezama to favor the descriptive element over the purely narrative element.[1] For some readers, however, *Paradiso* fails as a novel precisely because of this imbalance between description and narration. These realists feel that the author's untrammeled pursuit of images sacrifices the flow of the narrative, and one particularly unsympathetic critic, J. M. Alonso, concludes that Lezama's style, "is an openly Dandyish cult of cultivations, unashamedly filled with long, elliptical sentences featuring a distinctly self-congratulatory inclination for the most learned if not arcane choices where simpler ones seem quite possible."[2] Despite the unfavorable verdict that Alonso's description is designed to elicit, few devotees of the Cuban writer would quibble about the accuracy of his characterization of Lezama's prose. They, however, would assign a positive value to the same traits of style that Alonso considers glaring flaws. What is at issue here is a conflict between two aesthetic systems that are diametrically opposed. Alonso's formulation reveals that his unfavorable verdict is firmly grounded in the aesthetics of the realist novel whose canons are offended by the excesses of *Paradiso*. His remarks about the impact of the translation of Lezama's novel on the English reader leave no doubt about his aesthetic presuppositions: "Unfortunately, rendered into English, I believe it [Lezama's style] only succeeds in offending a puritanism that has progressively been dominating English writing since the days of the Royal Academy of Science and its battle against the Metaphysicals" ("A Sentimental Realism," p. 46). Alonso apparently sees no reason to question the dominance of aesthetic puritanism.

Although Alonso criticizes Lezama for making all his characters (regardless of social class or education) "talk in floods of classical (n.b., European, quintessentially white) erudition" (p. 46), a fact which in my opinion would seem to indicate the author's conscious departure from the conventions of realism, he reaches the conclusion that Lezama is a realist and a bad one at that. According to Alonso, Lezama "seriously pretends to convince us that his *Paradiso* was not any such artificial paradise, some purely literary realm, but rather the world as it was to his experience, filtered for us by his love for it. In a word, reality. Therefore, despite his Gongorist, Decadentist plumage, Lezama turns out to be merely a kind of sentimental Realist" (p. 47).

Another critic who arrives at a negative evaluation of Lezama's style is Julio Rodríguez-Luis. He reaches this position via a different route and with very different values from Alonso, but his discomfort with Lezama's project also hinges primarily on the issue of realism: "Perhaps because the world of *Paradiso* and its author himself are very close to me, it is more difficult for me than for other readers to accept his continuous ornamentation of reality. Despite the more or less brilliant or original images that attempt to transcend it, I continue to see a squalid petit-bourgeois reality which is not accepted as such and whose interest, therefore, is not transmitted (as would happen, for example, in a true realist novel) from the man Lezama to us."[3] Although Rodríguez-Luis is willing to contemplate the argument that Lezama was not interested in the novel as a genre, he perceives a fundamental contradiction in the execution of *Paradiso*. For Rodríguez-Luis, Lezama is still a practitioner of the realist novel *malgré lui:* "What characterizes the novel *Paradiso* is, therefore, the effort to express daily experience on a plane capable of transcending it, enhancing it so as to transform it into pure art—hence the similarity with Góngora's poetry. Nevertheless, that experience per se attracts the author, and its reproduction dominates the writing, a fact which in the final analysis is perfectly consistent with the nature of the novel as a genre" (*La literatura hispanoamericana*, p. 103). Lezama's interest in daily life and the biographical structure of *Paradiso*, according to Rodríguez-Luis, betray a rather traditional novelistic intent beneath the protestations of the new poetics of Cemí-Lezama. He therefore argues that *Paradiso* ultimately cannot be judged except as a novel. Having established his right to apply the conventions of the novel, Rodríguez-Luis compares *Paradiso* to other twentieth-century works that also employ an autobiographical structure to chronicle the development of an artistic vocation:

> In Proust's major novel, which is in large measure autobiographical and which, like *Paradiso*, also concludes with the definition of an artistic vocation, the attention to social, psychological, and physical reality is absorbing. However, while Proust explains and analyzes daily life in all its minutiae only in relation to the feelings and ideas of his protagonist, Lezama's commentary weaves around reality a border of metaphors whose intention is not interpretive but ornamental. He is interested in daily reality itself insofar as it evokes his own biography, and not, like the novelists of modernity, in memory (Proust), language (Joyce), conscience (Svevo), ethical, philosophical, and cultural problems (Kafka, Mann, Gide, Musil). Lezama limits himself to decorating his reproduction of reality, to poeticizing it—which is not the same thing as transcending it. (p. 104)

Far from contributing to the renovation of the genre, Rodríguez-Luis concludes, *Paradiso* is in essence a novel cast in a pre-Proustian mold.

Although different in approach and scope, the two negative reactions discussed are characterized by the persistence of the aesthetic paradigm of realism. Alonso's brief note evinces an almost hostile attitude toward the "excesses" of Lezama's prose and decries the author's alleged inability to fulfill the demands of novelistic verisimilitude. Alonso finds fault with the portrayal of the characters and, in

general, with the vision of life depicted in *Paradiso* because he im-
putes a realistic intention to its author. Unlike Alonso, who makes
no attempt to justify his application of the standards of realism to an
author who has never expressed his allegiance to that literary banner, Rodríguez-Luis examines the structure of *Paradiso* in the light
of the claims made by Lezama's poetics and finds that the execution
of the novel contradicts the author's program. The tension he feels
between the autobiographical material and the poetic proclamations
in *Paradiso* leads him to diagnose a bad—though unwitting—case
of crypto-realism. For Rodríguez-Luis the failure of *Paradiso* and, in
fact, many traits of Lezama's style are symptomatic of Latin American cultural underdevelopment.[4] By focusing on the problematic
tension between the poetics of José Cemí-Lezama and the apparent
realistic motivation of *Paradiso,* Rodríguez-Luis's dissenting voice
has rendered no small service.

Despite the coherence of his argument, I find Rodríguez-Luis's
final, negative evaluation of *Paradiso* unacceptable. Due to *Paradiso's* essential heterogeneity and its author's evident insouciance
regarding genre distinctions, any reading that employs realism as a
perspective, even in its modern and postmodern manifestations,
tends to produce an a priori condemnation of the novel. However
well-intentioned and rigorous, any such reading ultimately becomes
a perverse exercise that does little to explain *Paradiso's* significant
contributions to Latin American literature and its impact on readers' future expectations about fictive genres.

Concluding that *Paradiso* is a botched realist novel will not make
it go away. It seems more constructive and fruitful to consider *Paradiso* within the tradition of carnivalization and the dialogical novel.
On the other hand, a danger inherent in such an approach is to make
ideological claims for the novel that a close examination might not
sustain. When *Paradiso* is considered in the light of the characteristics of the dialogical novel described by the Russian theorist Mikhail
Bakhtin, the rich promise as well as the limits of this approach become evident. The Bakhtinian reading of *Paradiso* has sought to re-
mind readers that the conventions of realism do not exhaust the possibilities of the novel. Emir Rodríguez Monegal responded to the
early objections laid against *Paradiso* by observing that it was being
judged inappropriately. Instead of expecting *Paradiso* to conform to
the tradition of realism, he suggested that the novel be examined in
the light of a different and equally important tradition represented
by Petronius's *Satyricon,* Rabelais's *Gargantua and Pantagruel,* Cer-
vantes's *Don Quixote,* and Sterne's *Tristram Shandy*—the carnival-
esque, dialogical novel.[5]

Rodríguez Monegal's suggestion is motivated precisely by the desire to resolve the apparent contradiction between the conservative and the innovative aspects of the novel, the parodic and autobiographical aspects that realist critics see as a major flaw. For him Bakhtin's concepts of carnivalization and the dialogical novel permit this resolution: ". . . the Lezaman jesting and parody would not be seen as something extravagant which invades an autobiographical family novel and destroys it, but as the most explicit sign possible of that poetic reality which is (like that of the carnival) at the same time celebration and blasphemy, exaltation and jeer, consecration and destruction" (*"Paradiso:* Una silogística," p. 533). Rodríguez Monegal's remarks offer a fresh theoretical context for the evaluation of Lezama's novel. In the new context established by the Bakhtinian reading, the values of homogeneity and closure, predominant in realism, are displaced by heterogeneity and open-endedness. The virtue of this critical perspective on Lezama's work is readily apparent. It is not difficult to draw the analogy between the critical reception of Dostoevsky's novels and that of *Paradiso*. The Russian and the Cuban novelist immediately present problems from the viewpoint of genre. Bakhtin argues (as I have attempted to demonstrate in the case of Lezama) that the root of the problem lies in applying to Dostoevsky a set of literary conventions that are not only irrelevant but that actually obscure his contribution—the creation of the dialogical novel. The charges leveled at the Russian novelist are similar to those brought against Lezama: "From the viewpoint of a consistently monologic visualization and understanding of the represented world, from the viewpoint of some monologic canon for the proper construction of novels, Dostoevsky's world may seem a chaos, and the construction of his novels some sort of conglomerate of disparate materials and incompatible principles for shaping them. Only in the light of Dostoevsky's fundamental artistic task, which we will formulate here, can one begin to understand the profound organic cohesion, consistency and wholeness of Dostoevsky's poetics."[6] Bakhtin dismisses the relevance of the previous canon for the proper construction of novels because he believes that Dostoevsky has in fact created a new genre. For the Russian theorist, the heart of his novelist's contribution—also the chief source of critical confusion—is the creation of a type of novel that captures a multi-voicedness. According to him, this polyphony was fundamentally misunderstood as critics tried in vain to isolate a single voice amid the chorus of voices that would speak for Dostoevsky: "Out of the concrete and integral consciousnesses of the characters (and of the author himself) they surgically removed ideological theses, which they either arranged in a dynamic dialectical series or juxtaposed to one another as absolute and irreducible antinomies. The interaction of several unmerged consciousnesses was replaced by an interrelationship of ideas, thoughts, and attitudes gravitating toward a single consciousness" (*Problems of Dostoevsky's Poetics*, p. 9). The resulting contradictory readings of the novels are taken by Bakhtin as proof of his contention that what exists in Dostoevsky's works is a "plurality of equally authoritative ideological positions" (p. 18).

The principal innovations of Dostoevsky's dialogical novel are its refusal to employ characters as illustrations for a sermon, the primacy of space over time, and the absence of finalization. These Bakhtin opposes to the monological novel's "homophonic evolution of a single consciousness" (p. 32), the primacy of time over space, and philosophical finalization.

When we undertake the examination of *Paradiso* in terms of the characteristics described by Bakhtin, it appears to share many more traits of the monologic Romantic novel than the dialogical Dostoevskian novel. In fact, Bakhtin's description of the pattern of the Romantic novel seems to fit *Paradiso* rather well: "From the pathos of personality in the worldview of the author, a direct transition to the real-life pathos of the characters, and from there back again for a monologic conclusion by the author: this is the typical path taken by a monologic novel of the romantic type. . . . It is precisely the Romantics who in the very reality they depict give direct expression to their own artistic sympathies and evaluations, all the while objectifying and turning into a material thing all they cannot mark with the accent of their own voice" (p. 12).

A comparison of Dostoevsky's and Lezama's treatment of their characters is illuminating in this respect. The first impression the reader has in Lezama's novel is that, as in Dostoevsky, the authorial viewpoint arises from the polyphony of voices created by José Cemí, Eugenio Foción and Ricardo Fronesis. Nothing, however, could be further from the truth. Although, as many critics of *Paradiso* have correctly asserted, the three can be taken to represent different aspects of the adolescent personality, different paths to follow in life, they, unlike Dostoevsky's characters, do not represent equally authoritative ideological positions. It cannot be said of Lezama, as Bakhtin says of Dostoevsky, that "not a single one of the ideas of the heroes—neither the "negative" nor the "positive" heroes—becomes a principle of authorial representation, and none constitute the novelistic world in its entirety" (p. 25). Every reader of *Paradiso* will remember the lengthy dialogues of the three young men on varied philosophical and theological issues (in Chapters 9, 10, and 11), but they are, in fact, closer to a Socratic model than to the Dostoevskian concept of dialogue as described by Bakhtin. Although Bakhtin places the Socratic dialogue among the ancestors of the dialogical novel, the *spoudogeloios* ("serious-smiling") genres, he stresses the mono-logic, dialectical character assumed by the Socratic dialogues: "We emphasize that Socratic notions of the dialogic nature of truth lay at the folk-carnivalistic base of the genre of Socratic dialogue, deter-mining its *form*, but they did not by any means always find expres-sion in the actual content of the individual dialogues. The content often assumed a monologic character that contradicted the form-shaping idea of the genre" (p. 110). For the Russian theorist dialogue entails a juxtaposition though never a resolution of the voices, while in *Paradiso* it is Cemí's voice—clearly identified with the author's—that predominates in the end, as the total disappearance of his friends from the novel indicates.

The contrast in the treatment of the characters is related to a basic difference in the authors' strategies. According to Bakhtin:

> The fundamental category of Dostoevsky's mode of artistic visualizing was not evolution, but *coexistence* and *interaction*. He saw and con-ceived his world primarily in terms of space, not time. . . . An artist such as Goethe, for example, gravitates organically toward an evolving sequence. . . . In contrast to Goethe, Dostoevsky attempted to perceive the very stages themselves in their *simultaneity*, to *juxtapose* and *counterpose* them dramatically, and not stretch them out into an evolv-ing sequence. For him, to get one's bearings on the world meant to con-ceive all its contents as simultaneous, and *to guess at their inter-relationships in the cross-section of a single moment.* (p. 28)

Chapter 2 shows that in a different sense and at the level of his prose style Lezama privileges space over time. But in the sense employed by Bakhtin, *Paradiso* is ultimately concerned with evolution and not with focusing on simultaneous relationships. This is necessarily the case because of its structure as a *Bildungsroman*. Beyond the ex-igencies of the *Bildungsroman*, *Paradiso*'s stress on the evolution of an all-encompassing consciousness (Cemí's) reflects Lezama's desire for philosophical finalization.[7]

In this respect, Lezama also approaches a Romantic attitude re-jected by Dostoevsky toward "the contradictory evolution of the hu-man spirit, very much in keeping with the Hegelian idea."[8] In effect, the three friends, Fronesis, Foción, and Cemí clearly play out a He-gelian dialectic. The phrase Rodríguez Monegal employs to describe the three friends, "dialectical trinity" (p. 530), brilliantly captures both aspects of the configuration created by Lezama. Just as the Trinity is defined as three persons in one God, Fronesis, Foción, and Cemí are conceived not as separate characters but as a composite protagonist. At the same time, however, the triple constellation is only temporary. The thesis put forth in the characterization of Fronesis is juxtaposed by his antithesis, Foción, and is finally resolved in the characterization of Cemí, who becomes a synthesis of his friends. Lezama's characterization of Cemí is, as shown in Chapter 3, designed to find an ideological solution to the conflict between Fronesis and Foción.

Examination of *Paradiso* in the light of Bakhtin's concept of the dialogical novel reveals that in several important features Lezama's work is actually closer in spirit to the monologic novel. It remains to be seen if it indeed partakes of the *carnival sense of the world.*

Bakhtin places Dostoevsky's dialogical novel within the tradition of what the ancient Greeks called the *spoudogeloios* ("serious-smiling") genres.[9] These genres, which are rather diverse, always display a carnival sense of the world that "determines their basic features and places image and word in them in a special relationship to reality" (p. 107). Of the three characteristics he gives for the seriocomical realm in literature, only the third one is pertinent to Lezama's novels:

> A third characteristic is the deliberate multi-layered and hetero-voiced nature of all these genres. They reject the stylistic unity (or better, the single-styled nature) of the epic, the tragedy, high rhetoric, the lyric. Characteristic of these genres are a multi-toned narration, the mixing of high and low, serious and comic; they make wide use of inserted genres—letters, found manuscripts, retold dialogues, parodies on the high genres, parodically reinterpreted citations; in some of them we observe a mixing of prosaic and poetic speech, living dialects and jargons (and in the Roman stage, direct bilingualism as well) are introduced, and various authorial masks make their appearance. Alongside the representing word there appears the *represented* word; in certain genres a leading role is played by the double-voiced word. And what appears here, as a result, is a radically new relationship to the word as the material of literature. (p. 108)

It is in terms of this characteristic that a Bakhtinian perspective proves most useful in helping to situate Lezama's artistic contribution. Unquestionably monologic with regard to philosophical finalization, and the dominance of the authorial perspective over those of the characters, *Paradiso* nevertheless partakes of *the carnival sense of the world* when it comes to its "radically new relationship to the word as the material of literature."

"Serious-smiling" is the most appropriate epithet to encompass the contradictory tone and narrative strategy that have confused so many readers and critics of Lezama. Here is the explanation for the incongruities of style and content that have been lamented or derided by readers who saw them as proof of the author's idiosyncratic education or ridiculous pomposity. To the *spoudogeloios* tradition belong the mixed genres that clash with each other in *Paradiso:* the *Bildungsroman* and the family novel; hermetic poetry and naïve narrative; the high-level language employed to describe the making of a custard or a squabble with the servants; an encyclopedic discourse that combines archaic language, philosophical jargon from diverse times and cultures, colloquialisms, and Cubanisms, as well as words that are simply invented by the author; the inclusion of poems within the text (Fronesis's and Oppiano Licario's poems about Cemí); the oneiric narratives of Chapter 12; the parody of the Socratic dialogues in the philosophical discussions of Cemí, Fronesis, and Foción.

Although it performs the valuable service of discarding the realist paradigm and inserting *Paradiso* within a congenial literary tradition, the Bakhtinian reading of Lezama's novel fails on several important counts. Close examination of *Paradiso* in terms of Bakhtin's two principal concepts (the dialogical novel and the carnival sense of the world) reveals that strictly speaking Lezama's work tends toward the monological and that it shares only one of three characteristics necessary to partake of "the carnival sense of the world." Nevertheless, that characteristic, Lezama's "radically new relationship to the word as the material of literature" (p. 108), is a major feature of *Paradiso.*

Building on the insights of Bakhtin, a poststructuralist reading of *Paradiso* has stressed the radicality of Lezama's writing. Severo Sarduy is the source of this critical approach that highlights the parallels between Lezama's poetics and poststructuralist theory. In interviews, essays, and the parodies and pastiches of Lezama in his own novels, Sarduy has drawn our attention to the important role of the gap between signified and signifier, the concept of *dépense,* and the practice of intertextuality in *Paradiso.* In a letter to Lezama that appears at the conclusion of the study entitled "Dispersión: Falsas notas/Homenaje a Lezama," ("Dispersion: False Notes/Homage to Lezama") Sarduy has given a description that stresses the *spoudogeloios* aspect of *Paradiso:* "The notes that I include synthesize the most organized and vastest study that I have undertaken of your work. If in them I have systematically practiced collage—poems, the superimposition of other texts—, tangential approximation and parody, it has been in order to attempt, in the image of *Paradiso*, a plurality of voices so as to elicit from that encounter the 'soft Cuban laughter' and with it break the monochord tone."[10] Likewise Sarduy has given a ground-breaking explanation of the role of cultural and historical allusions in Lezama's writing by stressing the importance of the "texture" of the represented word: ". . . on the Lezaman page what counts is not the veracity—in the sense of identity with something nonverbal—of the word, but its *dialogical presence*, its glitter. What counts is the texture *French, Latin, culture*, the chromatic value, the level they signify in the vertical cut of the writing, in its unfurling of parallel wisdom" (*Escrito sobre un cuerpo*, p. 63). The problem with Sarduy's approach, however, is that it negates the equally important role of the representing word in Lezama. *Paradiso* reflects an *equal* interest in the *representing* and the *represented* word. It is precisely because of this sustained double interest in the transparency and opaqueness of language that Lezama cannot be comfortably assimilated to a poststructuralist worldview that privileges the represented word, the texture of language, and the signifier over the representing word, the message, or the signified. It is totally comprehensible for one critic to read *Paradiso* as a crypto-realist novel, and for another to see a text that boldly embodies all the values of poststructuralist literary theory. Neither viewpoint totally represents Lezama's outlook. Although Sarduy, whose understanding of Lezama is profound, entertains no such distortion, he sometimes gives the impression that Lezama is a poststructuralist novelist *avant la lettre*. In the case of the family history and the *Bildungsroman* imbedded in *Paradiso*, however, it is clear that much more than the texture counts.

Sarduy himself is very aware of the partial image of Lezama that his commentaries propound. In "Dispersión" he preempts criticism of his formalistic bias by bringing forth a reader—"The (ever more hypothetical) reader of these pages"—who attacks him on this ground: "It seems to me that all this subtle scaffolding, so structural and so much *à la mode*, besides being an unpublishable rigamarole which is so full of gallicisms that one is only struck by the rare hispanisms, does not go beyond the exterior, the peel. The author, using increasingly noticeable buzzwords, speaks of nothing but the *form*. But, please, what about human content? And even more, what about Lezama's insular metaphysics, his Theology—of which he doesn't even say a word—, his Tellurism, his Transcendence? Come, now! What frivolity! What decadence!" (pp. 83–84). With characteristic legerdemain Sarduy "deals" with the issue of *Paradiso*'s content. His parody disarms his critics through ridicule and simultaneously absolves him of the charge that he has not said one word about the human content of Lezama's novel.

By dwelling on the more radical traits of Lezama's prose, Sarduy brings him closer to his own novels. His assimilation of Lezama's project to his own, his blurring of the significant formal and ideological boundaries that separate his novels from those of his literary father are ample proof of Sarduy's admiration but also of his ongoing necessarily parricidal dialogue with Lezama.[11] In this dialogue, following a practice cultivated by Lezama, Sarduy's assimilation at times comes to displace Lezama. Enrico Mario Santí has explained the thematic importance of Oedipus in *Paradiso* and the essentially parricidal nature of Lezama's writing—of all writing: "And that repetition as structure of the world and of consciousness includes especially being as a son, that is to say, the son as the de-centered repetition of the father, as a de-centering of the origin. To be a son, to be a copy different from the original, not to be 'wellborn,' to have a rash, to quote incorrectly, to write badly, Licario seems to have said, is not a crime. Parricide is not only inevitable, but in fact we perpetuate it at every moment. We are always already parricides."[12]

By direct reference, allusion, quotation, parody, and pastiche, Lezama is present in Sarduy's novels, but *De donde son los cantantes* (*From Cuba with a Song*), *Cobra, Maitreya,* and *Colibrí* (*Hummingbird*) undermine the role of the representing word to a degree unknown in Lezama's writing and with a very different object. Consciously (premeditatively) they enact the carnival sense of the world. Sarduy's novels always exist in a carnival time, but, unlike Lezama's carnival, which exists in counterpoint to Lent and Easter, Sarduy's exists out of context or rather is its own context. For this very reason Sarduy's novels, paradoxically, do not fully embrace (as do *Paradiso* and *Oppiano Licario*) the *spoudogeloios* perspective. The tension between the serious and the comical, fundamental to Lezama's worldview, becomes tactical in Sarduy.

Philosophy, religion, history, and culture appear in the novels of Sarduy in order to be debunked and replaced by other avatars which in turn will also be undermined by the author's various ironical strategies.[13] Cultural content is the raw material used by Sarduy to dramatize a philosophical relativism, which, giving another turn to the screw, he parodies in the last words of *Maitreya:* "Adoptaron otros dioses, águilas. Mimaron ritos hasta la idiotez o el hastío. Para demostrar la impermanencia y vacuidad de todo." ("They adopted other gods, eagles. They mimed rites unto idiocy or boredom. In order to demonstrate the impermanence and vacuousness of everything.")[14] The tension between serious and comical components in Sarduy's novels is strategic, provisional, and always ends in derision. Roberto González Echevarría's precise characterization of Sarduy's project outlines its parallels with poststructuralist thought: "In Sarduy's system, writing is not preceded by signification or by presence, but by writing itself. Except that that writing, or as Derrida calls it, *archiécriture*, composed of negations of differences or *différances* (deferrals in a temporal and spatial sense), installs itself precisely as the absent origin that the text produces through the ruptures of its negations."[15]

In Lezama the consistent tension between the serious and the comical arises from a mystical, as well as an aesthetic imperative to seek and to sustain a precarious equilibrium between the proliferating, often opaque, *represented word* and the equally necessary *representing word* whose task is to bear witness. Lezama's style in his poetry and his prose is fundamentally preoccupied with the harnessing of obscurity to the task of mystical illumination.

I have chosen to dwell on Lezama's search for this precarious equilibrium. Chapters 2 and 3 respectively examine how Lezama conceives of that double aesthetical and ethical challenge in *Paradiso*. Chapter 4 studies the practice of reading and writing as cultural consumption described in Lezama's essays, and Chapter 5 illustrates his faith in the epiphanic character of literary activity, whether creative or critical, by focusing on a remarkable passage of *Paradiso*. Finally, Chapter 6 seeks to place Lezama in the context of contemporary literature by examining the validity of the analogy traced by Julio Cortázar in a well-known essay and by Lezama himself in *Oppiano Licario* between his work and that of the French painter Henri Rousseau. Lezama's very personal interpretation of Rousseau the man and the painter contains a surprising response directed at both his adherents and critics. Lezama's consideration of his own poetics filtered through Henri Rousseau will bring us full circle to answer the major question raised in this introduction: How should Lezama be read?

Chapter 2
· · · · · · ·

The Aesthetics of Excess:
The Novel as Fibroma

Only God is enough.
        —*St. Theresa of Avila, "Nada te turbe"*

*I say this so that young people will insist on what they
don't comprehend, so that they will return to what they
don't understand, because in the end their eyes will open
upon a marvelous world.*
        —*José Lezama Lima*

*[Lezama,] you are seated on a chair made of a single
cloud of polysemous metal wrenched from the avarice of
the dictionary.*
        —*Octavio Paz, "Refutación de los espejos"*

· · ·

T he principle of sustained contradiction lies at the very core of
Lezama's aesthetics. Driven by a stubborn faith that often invokes Tertullian's "Certum est, quia impossibile est" ("It is
certain because it is impossible"), Lezama's poetic practice consists
in knowingly attempting the impossible. Despite its apparent mean-
dering, *Paradiso* leads José Cemí inexorably to the moment when he
will understand and willingly embrace the challenge left him by
his Virgil, Oppiano Licario. As Lezama himself puts it in his essay
"Confluencias" ("Confluences"), "todas las posibilidades del sistema poético han sido puestas en marcha, para que Cemí concurra a
la cita con Licario, el Icaro, el nuevo intentador de lo imposible"
(*Obras completas*, 2: 1217) ("all the possibilities of the poetic system have been set in motion so that Cemí will be present at the
appointment with Licario, the Icarus, the new attempter of the
impossible").
Lezama's style insistently seeks difficulties; it persists in batter-
ing the darkness. Strangely, however, his quest for hermeticism is
not motivated by the postmodern pessimism that sees language as a
prison house, but by a mystical belief in the miraculous power of
words to discover and to communicate truth.[1] Lezama's poetic practice consists of the search for images that will illuminate and gradually lead to ultimate enlightenment. As González Echevarría has ob-

served, "In his work Lezama aspires to the miracle—the incarnation of the word."[2] Although the terrain he chooses for that poetic practice is always the boundary between meaning and meaninglessness, the poetic act is for him a joyful affirmation. Paradoxically, therefore, the excesses of Lezama's prose are subservient to an underlying discipline, a dedication to stylistic difficulty, not for its own sake, but, as in the case of the *koan* of Zen Buddhism, for what the sudden confrontation with contradiction may reveal. A *koan* is the paradox that the Zen master, or *roshi*, assigns to his pupil. A well-known example is "We know what the sound of two hands clapping is like, but what is the sound of one hand clapping?" Like Lezama's images, which seek to create new connections, and thus a path to insight, the *koan* is "designed to break down the conceptualization superimposed on the flow of experience and to bring about intuitive insight."[3] The model of Zen Buddhism with its stress on spiritual discipline, sudden illuminations (*satori*) that are steps to Buddhahood, and particularly the essential relationship between the Zen master and his pupil is perhaps more important to Lezama than the Christian model exemplified in the relationship of the mystic and the father confessor. The great Spanish mystics, St. Theresa of Avila and St. John of the Cross, are present to an important degree in Lezama's writings, but in *Paradiso* the central relationship, that of José Cemí and Oppiano Licario, closely follows the Zen paradigm.[4] The last "*koan*" Oppiano Licario assigns his pupil is the poem José Cemí receives after his teacher's death, and it is largely this sonnet that precipitates the young man's insight at the end of the novel.[5]

The first words of Lezama's 1957 collection of essays, *La expresión americana* (*American Expression*), can be taken as his aesthetic manifesto:

> *Solo lo difícil es estimulante; solo la resistencia que nos reta es capaz de enarcar, suscitar y mantener nuestra potencia de conocimiento; pero, en realidad, ¿qué es lo difícil?, ¿lo sumergido, tan solo, en las maternales aguas de lo oscuro?, ¿lo originario sin causalidad, antítesis o logos? Es la forma en devenir en que un paisaje va hacia un sentido, una interpretación o una sencilla hermenéutica, para ir después hacia su reconstrucción, que es en definitiva lo que marca su eficacia o desuso, su fuerza ordenancista o su apagado eco, que es su visión histórica. (2: 279)[6]*

· · ·

Only what is difficult is stimulating; only the resistance that challenges us is capable of rearing up, of inciting and maintaining our potency for knowledge, but in truth, what is the difficult, only what is submerged in the maternal waters of darkness, what originates without causality, antithesis or *logos*? It is the form of becoming in which a landscape goes toward a meaning, an interpretation or a simple hermeneutics, in order to go later toward its reconstruction, which in the final analysis is what marks its efficacy or obsolescence, its ordering force or its extinguished echo, which is its historic vision.

Difficulty is stimulating not only in a sensual sense, but because it, like Socrates, is the midwife of enlightenment. Most striking of all in this passage is Lezama's clearly instrumental attitude toward difficulty. Obscurity for its own sake is categorically rejected because of its lack of causality or *logos*, which Lezama always employs in the Stoic sense reflected in the gospel of St. John, meaning reason for being. Difficulty is, therefore, valued for its dialectical power, its ability to interpret, to reconstruct. For Lezama, its ultimate efficacy or uselessness depends upon these virtues.

Several critics, and Lezama himself, have declared that along with its obscurities *Paradiso* contains the keys to its interpretation. Emir Rodríguez Monegal has eloquently expressed this paradoxical aspect of Lezama's novel: ". . . before a text like that of *Paradiso* the irresistible temptation arises to declare it obscure, incomprehensible, absurd. The paradox is that few books like *Paradiso* have such a power of luminous irradiation; few texts contain their own gloss up to such a point of total saturation; few fictions develop as this one does the spiral of their configurations with such a sure intuition of the road traveled and yet to travel."[7] *Paradiso* is seeded with privileged episodes that not only guide José Cemí to the threshold of his poetic vocation but actually teach its readers how to read the novel.

Although Lezama's critics inexplicably have not given it the attention it deserves, Chapter 10 contains a passage that in my opinion surpasses all others in hermeneutic potential. I refer to the series of analogies employed by Lezama to describe the seventeen-pound fibroma extracted from Rialta, José Cemí's mother.[8] Like the exhortation of Cemí's mother, the near drownings of Cemí and his sister, the game of jacks, Uncle Alberto's letter, the chess game, and the vision of the horses and the Roman procession, the extraction of the fibroma is a privileged episode—and it is the one that presents Cemí's most important epiphany.[9] The passage is a typical linguistic episode of *Paradiso*, but its self-reflective character accords it a special status for anyone concerned with the aesthetics of Lezama's novel. This second lesson that springs from the protagonist's mother (in this case literally) is the most complete and forceful statement of novelistic aesthetics in *Paradiso*.

In order to appreciate its importance, the episode of the fibroma must be placed in the context of Cemí's poetic apprenticeship. In particular it must be understood in the light of the first lesson, the key incident in Chapter 9 in which Cemí, after his introduction to the adult world of the university and his first brush with danger— the political riot between the students and the police—is called to the vocation of poetry by his mother.

The main purpose of Rialta's oration is to teach her son to discern between sterile risks and those that will bear spiritual fruit. She consecrates him to the type of danger that will lead to an epiphany:

> *Oyeme lo que te voy a decir: No rehúses el peligro, pero intenta siempre lo más difícil. Hay el peligro que enfrentamos como una sustitución, hay también el peligro que intentan los enfermos, ese es el peligro que no engendra ningún nacimiento en nosotros, el peligro sin epifanía. Pero cuando el hombre, a través de sus días, ha intentado lo más difícil, sabe que ha vivido en peligro, aunque su existencia haya sido silenciosa, aunque la sucesión de su oleaje haya sido manso, sabe que ese día que le ha sido asignado para su transfigurarse, verá, no los peces dentro del fluir, lunarejos en la movilidad, sino los peces en la canasta estelar de la eternidad.* (1: 321)

• • •

> Listen to what I'm going to tell you: Don't reject danger and always try what is most difficult. There's a danger that [we confront] in the form of substitution, there's also a danger that sick people seek out, a sterile danger, the danger without epiphany. But when a man throughout his days has tested what is most difficult, he knows that he has lived in danger, and even though [his] existence has been silent, even though the succession of its waves has been peaceful, he knows that a day has been assigned to him in which he will be transfigured, and he will not see the fish inside the current, dappled in motion, but the fish in the starry basket of eternity. (*Paradiso*, trans. Rabassa, p. 228)

The passage contains all the important topoi that will recur throughout the novel in the context of José Cemí's poetic and spiritual progress: the spiritual utility of certain dangers, the concept of epiphany, the idea of a final transfiguration, and the opposition of fluidity (associated with mortality and transitoriness) to "la fijeza" (the stasis of immortality). It is also, clearly, the source of the dual (aesthetical and ethical) vision that guides José Cemí's poetical quest, as well as Lezama's poetic practice in *Paradiso*.

The decisive impact of the young man's interview with his mother is assiduously underscored by Lezama. The whole of the episode, which recalls the dedication of the prophet Samuel to the service of God by his mother (1 Samuel 1) and the relationship of St. Monica and St. Augustine, is highlighted by the aura of religion. Rialta, who receives José Cemí with rosary in hand, invokes the aid of the Holy Spirit to find the words that she knows she must speak to her son:

> *Mientras esperaba tu regreso, pensaba en tu padre y pensaba en ti, re-*
> *zaba el rosario y me decía: ¿Qué le diré a mi hijo cuando regrese de ese*
> *peligro? El paso de cada cuenta del rosario, era el ruego de que una vo-*
> *luntad secreta te acompañase a lo largo de la vida, que siguieses un*
> *punto, una palabra, que tuvieses siempre una obsesión que te llevase*
> *siempre a buscar lo que se manifiesta y lo que se oculta. Una obsesión*
> *que nunca destruyese las cosas, que buscase en lo manifestado lo*
> *oculto, en lo secreto lo que asciende para que la luz lo configure. Eso es*
> *lo que siempre pido para ti y lo seguiré pidiendo mientras mis dedos*
> *puedan recorrer las cuentas de un rosario. Con sencillez yo le pedía esa*
> *palabra al Padre y al Espíritu Santo, a tu padre muerto y al espíritu*
> *vivo, pues ninguna madre, cuando su hijo regresa del peligro, debe de*
> *decirle una palabra inferior.* (1: 320–321)
>
> . . .
>
> Waiting for you to come home, I was thinking about your father and thinking about you, saying my rosary and asking myself: 'What will I tell my son when he comes back from that danger?' The passing of each rosary bead was a prayer for a secret will to go with you all through your life, [for you to follow a point, a word,] for you always to have [an obsession] that would [always] bring you to seek what [manifests itself and what hides itself. An obsession] that would never destroy [things], that would look for the hidden in the [manifested, in the secret what rises up] for the light to give it form. That's what I always ask [for you], and I'll go on asking for it as long as my fingers can run over the beads of a rosary. [With simplicity] I asked for [that] word from the Father and the Holy Spirit, from your dead father and the living spirit, [because] no mother, when her son returns from danger, should ever say any [base word] to him. (pp. 227–228)

Thus, we begin with a strong suggestion that her words are divinely inspired. True to her name, which echoes the Rialto bridge in Venice, she serves as a bridge between her son and God. After she utters the message, Lezama, as if to leave no stone unturned, intervenes with his own voice in order to confer unequivocably upon Rialta's words a status akin to that of sacred scripture: "Sé que esas son las palabras más hermosas que Cemí oyó en su vida, después de las que leyó en los Evangelios, y que nunca oirá otras que lo pongan tan de-

cisivamente en marcha" (1: 322) ("I know that those are the most
beautiful words Cemí ever heard in his life after the ones he read in
the Gospels and that he will never hear any others that will so de-
cisively set him in motion" [p. 228]). The dizzying momentary col-
lapse of boundaries attests to the privileged status Lezama accords
to the entire episode. In this passage Rialta's words, themselves, reflect the type of mystical transfiguration she sees as Cemí's ultimate
logos (reason for being). The relationship of analogy between the
Trinity and the Cemí family momentarily becomes one of identity.
By the power of a pun and syntactical apposition, God the Father becomes the dead father (Colonel Cemí), and the Holy Spirit is translated into the living spirit of the dead father within the family, and
within Cemí. Ultimately the living spirit of the dead father survives
in Lezama's own act of writing, because in this passage the always
tenuous boundary between novel and autobiography, between José
Cemí and José Lezama Lima, is also erased. This conflation of fiction
and reality is addressed in the text itself by Lezama's use of the testi-
monial, "I know that those are the most beautiful words Cemí ever
heard," but even more openly by the text's insistence on the historical reality of Rialta's words and the curious expectation (voiced by
Rialta) that they will be considered fictitious: "Algunos impostores
pensarán que yo nunca dije estas palabras, que tú las has inven-
cionado, pero cuando tú des la respuesta por el testimonio, tú y yo
sabremos que sí las dije y que las diré mientras viva y que tú las
seguirás diciendo después que me haya muerto" (1: 322). ("Some
[impostors] will think that I never said these words, that you invented them, but when you give the answer [by means of] the testi-
mony, you and I will know that I did say them and that I will say
them as long as I live and that you will continue saying them after I
have died" [p. 228].) Rialta's words, thanks to her protestations, leave
the realm of fiction to become those of Rosa Lima, the author's
mother. In the face of an autobiographical incident of the greatest
personal transcendence, Lezama abruptly dispenses with the limita-
tions of fiction. This passage creates a *mise en abîme*. Its subject
matter is José Cemí's dedication to a poetic quest seen as a "testi-
mony," but the authorial perspective that is suddenly thrust upon
the text reveals that it simultaneously chronicles the author's turning point, his acceptance of his mother's challenge to embrace a
fruitful obsession for life. At this crucial point in the novel Lezama
saw as the ultimate fulfillment of that challenge—of that filial obligation—the author feels compelled to abandon the conventions of
fiction. He "bears witness" in his own voice, briefly restoring the dialogue with his now dead mother. The text, then, *does* what it *says*.

After this exhortation, Cemí's mother once more (and this time unexpectedly) plays a role in his education when she undergoes surgery. The enormous fibroma, dangerous fruit of his mother's body, unexpectedly provides the occasion for Cemí's discovery of his creative mission. Through the contemplation of the fibroma and its physiological effects on his mother's organism, he discovers the type of artistic danger that will lead him to a new poetic harmony—the obsession that will give direction to his life. In this manner Lezama establishes a fundamental analogy that equates the development of the fibroma with the strategy Cemí will follow in his poetic quest, a process that his very prose seeks to embody.

The actual description of the fibroma, fascinating for what it reveals of the building blocks of Lezama's prose style, merits quotation in full and a detailed analysis:

Dentro de una vasija transparente, como una olla de cristal, se encontraba el fibroma del tamaño de un jamón grande. En las partes de la vasija donde se apoyaba, el tejido se amorataba por la más pronta detención de la sangre. El resto del fibroma mostraba todavía tejidos bermejos, debilitados hasta el rosa o crecidos a un rojo horno. Algunas estrías azules se distinguían del resto de aquella sobrante carnación, cobrando como una cabrilleante coloración de arcoiris, rodeado de nubes todavía presagiosas. Los tejidos por donde había resbalado el bisturí, lucían más abrillantados, como si hubiesen sido acariciados por el acero en su más elaborada fineza de penetración. En su fragmento visible semejaba una península recortada de un mapa, con sus huellas eruptivas, los extraños recorridos de la lava, sus arrogancias orográficas y sus treguas de deslizamiento hidrográfico. Aquellas insensibles fibras parecían, dentro de la vasija de cristal, un dragón atravesado por una lanza, por un rayo de luz, por una hebra de energía capaz de destruir esas minas de cartón y de carbón, extendiéndose por sus galerías como una mano que se va abriendo hasta dejar inscripciones indescifrables en paredones oscilantes, como si su base estuviese aconsejada por los avances y retrocesos de las aguas de penetración coralina, somnolientas, que llegan hasta montes estallantes del apisonado de la noche húmeda y metálica. El fibroma parecía todavía un coral vivaz en su arborescencia subterránea. (1: 451−452)

• • •

Inside a transparent vessel, a kind of crystal pot, was the fibroma, the size of a large ham. In the part of the vessel where it was resting, the tissue was turning purple with the more rapid detention of blood there. The rest of the fibroma still showed bright red tissue, weakened into pink or growing into an oven red. Some blue strips stood out from the

rest of that excess flesh, collecting the white-capped coloration of a rainbow surrounded by still ominous clouds. The tissues through which the
scalpel had slipped appeared more polished, as if it had been caressed by
the steel in its most [elaborate] delicacy of penetration. In its visible
fragment it resembled a peninsula cut out of a map, with its eruptive
traces, strange lava flows, its orographic arrogances and its truces of hy-
drographic slides. Those unfeeling fibers inside the glass jar looked like
a dragon run through by a lance, by a ray of light, by a thread of energy
capable of destroying those mines of cardboard and carbon, extending
through its galleries like a hand that goes along opening, until it [leaves]
undecipherable inscriptions on oscillating walls, as if its base were ad-
vised by the advances and retreats of the waters of coral penetration,
[sleepy,] which reach [bursting hills of] the tamped-down surface of the
damp and metallic night. The fibroma still looked like a coral [vivid] in
its subterranean arborescence. (p. 322)

When we finish reading the passage and come up for air, we observe that the description proper with its medical terms—*tejidos*
(tissues), *bisturí* (scalpel), *fibras* (fibers)—is interwoven with series
of comparisons that allude to different codes. These begin concretely,
though strangely enough, by alluding to a culinary code: the glass jar
is likened to a cooking pot and the fibroma itself to a large ham. Up
to this point, however, the comparisons are strictly utilitarian, helping the reader visualize the type of container and the size of the tumor. Although they always use an identifiable physical feature as
their point of departure, the analogies become increasingly intricate
and subjective as the prose acquires momentum. Thus certain blue
strands on the fibroma suggest a rainbow, but when that allusion, in
turn, evokes the image of ominous rainclouds, Lezama has taken us
very far from the actual description of benign tissue in a glass container. At this point, the author repeats the procedure, returning to a
depiction of the scalpel's marks on the fibroma. The cutting of the
surgical instrument and the description of a fragment of the growth
suggests a peninsula cut from a map, which then establishes the geo-
graphical/topographical code of the images that follow: traces of
eruptions, lava, bodies of water, etc. Lezama once more invokes the
point of departure, the fibers in the glass container, and launches the
final, most subjective and breathtaking configuration of images. The
fibroma is said to resemble a dragon pierced by a lance. The weapon
then becomes a ray of light, in turn suggesting energy. The thought
of energy coupled with the still resonating topographical imagery
yields the image of coal mines, flowing water, and coral reefs.
    Lezama's style depends on a deliberate ebb and flow between the

horizontal (syntagmatic) progress of the description of the tumor as Cemí's eye passes over it and the vertical (paradigmatic) stacks of images evoked by its physical features.[10] This ebb and flow between the progress of the description and the images the tumor elicits in Cemí's mind repeats the narrative dynamics of *Paradiso* as a whole. Lezama's characteristic strategy throughout the novel is to cultivate description at the expense of narration. The author returns to his narrative task only when the demands of description are satisfied. Likewise in this passage, the description of the fibroma, which defers the narration of Cemí's visit to his recovering mother, is in turn staggered to permit the inclusion of poetic imagery.

In order to characterize Lezama's strategy, I have employed the images of breathlessness and coming up for air.[11] Every return to the point of departure momentarily reaffirms the narrative flow imperiled by his digressions, but Lezama will catch his breath only long enough to make further digressions possible. This dangerous strategy recreates the anxiety of asthma that comes with every breath exhaled, the anxiety caused by the fear that the rhythm of breath will be broken. Aware of the perils this strategy entails for his prose, Lezama nevertheless insists in stretching the generic limits to the breaking point.

Cemí's meditations, which follow the description of the fibroma, flesh out the analogy between its growth and the aesthetic tenets that underlie the project of *Paradiso*. Rich in complexity, the analogy, strictly speaking, does not equate the fibroma to Lezama's prose style. Instead it suggests a comparison between the fibroma's physiological impact on the human organism and the consequences of a proliferating prose style on the equilibrium demanded by the generic conventions of the novel. The ambiguity of the fibroma is essential for Lezama; the growth of the fibroma results in a pathological condition that is at the same time an attempt at a cure—an effort to restore harmony. The aortic sclerosis and the ventricular hypertrophy result from the organism's attempt to reestablish the equilibrium upset by the proliferating fibroma. Likewise, although the fibroma is a threat to life, it must be irrigated with blood lest its putrefaction ensue and with it the death of the organism. Therefore, while the fibroma serves as an emblem of Lezama's style, it also reveals a self-awareness of the dangers entailed by his poetics. The passage plays with this ambiguity, dwelling on the conceits of a monstrosity and of an "abnormal normality":[12]

> *Las fibras que mostraban su sonroso hacían pensar en la esclerosis aórtica, cómo aquellas células se habían ido endureciendo y esclerosando*

*por un trabajo que las dañaba al estar destinado al enriquecimiento de
las células sobrantes, monstruosas, pero necesitadas también del riego
que evitaría la putrefacción de aquella monstruosidad derivada. De la
misma manera la hipertrofia ventricular izquierda se había formado
por el excesivo trabajo para satisfacer la demanda sanguínea del crecimiento progresivo de la adherencia. Aquellas diez y siete libras de
fibras inservibles le habían hecho al organismo una demanda peren-
toria como si se tratara de un sustitutivo logrado por el mismo cuerpo
para restablecer un equilibrio tan necesario como fatal. En la satisfac-
ción de aquella excrecencia, el organismo había tenido que destruir su
desarrollo normal, la simple estabilidad vital, de las más impotentes
vísceras. Deshecha la elasticidad aórtica, agrandando hasta el exceso el
ventrículo izquierdo, el organismo lograba emparejarse con el monstruo que lo habitaba. Para conseguir una normalidad sustitutiva, había
sido necesario crear nuevas anormalidades, con las que el monstruo
adherente lograba su normalidad anormal y una salud que se mantenía
a base de su propia destrucción.* (1: 452–453)*

* * *

The fibers that showed their blush made one think of aortic sclerosis,
how those cells had gone on hardening and becoming sclerotic with
labor that injured them, destined to the enrichment of the superfluous,
monstrous cells, but still needing the irrigation that would avoid the
putrefaction of that derivative monstrosity. In the same way, the ventricular hypertrophy had been created by excessive labor to satisfy the
blood demand of the progressive growth of the attachments. Those sev-
enteen pounds of useless fibers had made a peremptory demand on the
organism, a substitute made by the body itself to reestablishing a balance both necessary and fatal. In the satisfaction of that excrescence, the
organism had had to destroy normal development, the simple vital sta-
bility of [the most] impotent viscera. The aortic elasticity undone, the
left ventricle wildly expanding, the organism succeeded in [achieving
parity] with the monster that inhabited it. To find a substitute normality, it had been necessary to create new abnormalities by which the adherent monster attained its abnormal normality and a health that was
maintained on the basis of its own destruction. (p. 322)

Lezama pursues the fundamental paradox doggedly: it is an equilibrium as necessary as it is fatal, and the health of the organism is
maintained at the cost of its own destruction. The fibroma is the
monster with which the body must establish a dangerous balance.
This quest for an equilibrium which may turn out to be fatal is then
explicitly extended to the realm of literature:

*De la misma manera, en los cuerpos que logra la imaginación, hay que
destruir el elemento serpiente para dar paso al elemento dragón, un
organismo que está hecho para devorarse en el círculo, tiene que des-
truirse para que irrumpa una nueva bestia, surgiendo del lago sulfúrico,
pidiéndole prestadas sus garras a las grandes vultúridas y su cráneo al
can tricéfalo que cuida las moradas subterráneas. El fibroma tenía así
que existir como una monstruosidad que lograba en el organismo
nuevos medios de asimilación de aquella sorpresa, buscando un equilibrio más alto y más tenso.* (1: 453)

• • •

[In the same way, in the bodies achieved by imagination, it is necessary
to destroy the serpent element to make way for the dragon element, an
organism which is made to devour itself in the circle has to destroy
itself so that a new beast can take over, emerging from the sulphuric
lake, borrowing its claws from the great vultures and its cranium from
the three-headed dog that guards the subterranean dwellings. The fibroma, thus, had to exist as a monstrosity that attained in the organism
new means to assimilate that surprise, seeking a higher and tenser
equilibrium.]

This segment introduces the phrases *serpent element* and *dragon
element*, without whose interpretation the passage is unintelligible.
The study of this passage in the context of other similar ones in *Paradiso* and in particular Lezama's use of the *ouroboros*, the snake
that swallows its tail, permits a suggestive and coherent reading.
The key to the symbolism lies in the shapes of the two creatures:
the snake and the dragon. The dragon element is Lezama's artistic
desideratum; it represents a prose style characterized by the incrustation of imagery. The quest for a higher and tenser equilibrium,
entailed by the dragon element, is Lezama's retort to what he considers the sterile self-destruction of the realist novel where the serpent element—the single-minded pursuit of plot development—pre-
vails. The teleological drive of the realist novel leads it to eschew
any type of digression in order to speed the flow of the narrative toward its end—toward the resolution that is also the dissolution of
the novel. The linearity and morphological economy of the snake
represent the purely narrative element whose predominance ensures
safe passage to that telos (in the sense of both goal and end). In
Lezama's view, the realist narrative dominated by the serpent element is fashioned to swallow itself; its self-destruction leaves us in a
vacuum.[13] By a process of incrustation Lezama seeks to transform
the sterile and linear snake into a baroque serpent, a winged dragon

with three heads, leaving no room for doubt that the digressions and descriptive adherences are part and parcel of this rich abnormal normality.

What Lezama rejects, if it is possible to speak of rejection in the fundamentally inclusive *Paradiso,* is the very aesthetics of rejection that he sees in the realist conception of the novel.[14] It is curious that even the logic of his symbolism does not actually reject the snake of the linear narrative but, in accordance with a typical Lezaman strategy, incorporates it, assimilates it, transforms it into an ornate dragon.

The polymorphic metaphorical digressions and descriptions of *Paradiso* are neither ornamental in the traditional sense nor secondary; they are the primary strategies of Lezama's poetic practice. There is a fundamental difference between the value that he confers on description and that accorded to it by traditional rhetoric. Gérard Genette has explained the role played by lengthy description as a figure in traditional rhetoric: "It is known that traditional rhetoric places description under the same heading as the other figures of style, among the ornaments of discourse: extended and detailed description is considered as a pause and a recreation within the narrative; its role is purely aesthetic like that of sculpture in a classical building."[15] In the case of *Paradiso* something very different occurs. What Lezama demands from descriptions, more than the purely decorative effect mentioned by Genette (a judgment which entails a secondary role) is a way to detain the flow of the narrative so jealously protected by the aesthetics of realism. Genette's distinction between the effects of *narration* and *description* in a narrative helps us to appreciate the very special role of description (by which I mean all elements that do not further plot development) in *Paradiso:* ". . . narration is interested in actions or events as pure processes, and thereby places emphasis on the temporal and dramatic aspect of the narrative; description, on the contrary, because it lingers over objects and beings in their simultaneity, and views processes themselves as spectacles, seems to suspend the course of time and contributes to the disposition of the narrative in space" (*Figures II,* p. 59). The function of the narrative element in a tale is to create the effect of time while the descriptive element creates that of space. A novel in which description predominates over narration not only sacrifices the flow of the narrative but gives the impression that time has stopped.

Producing this impression of timelessness on the reader is one of the goals of Lezama's style, and he succeeds in freezing time thanks to his descriptive unrestraint. The lengthy descriptions, the series of analogies, the continuous metaphorical torrent are the instruments he employs in the practice of a type of alchemy—the alchemy of "la fijeza" (stasis). This is why Cemí thinks he sees, in the jar that contains his mother's fibroma, the *theion hudor* of the alchemists, "con su facultad de colorear los cuerpos sobre los que resbalaba con una lentitud invisible" (1: 453) ("with its faculty of coloring the bodies it slid over with an invisible slowness" [p. 323]). In alchemy, the *theion hudor* (divine water or sulphur water) is the substance that allows the transformation of base metals into noble metals, a transformation that according to Zosimos of Panopolis, the famous alchemist of the fourth century, requires their "death" and "resurrection."[16] For Lezama this becomes the death of the serpent and its resurrection as a dragon.

The dross of language if subjected to the proper procedure will render the gold of images, and it is through the poetic image that Lezama believes one can achieve immortality: first of all because the profusion of images can prolong the time of our reading by seemingly arresting it, and second because our persistent rubbing against the image will spark an illumination. In "Confluencias" Lezama conceives of this illumination in the religious terms of his heterodox Catholicism:

> *ya que el hombre es imagen, participa como tal y al final se encuentra con la aclaración total de la imagen, si la imagen le fuera negada desconocería totalmente la resurrección. La imagen es el incesante complementario de lo entrevisto y lo entreoído, el temible* entredeux *pascaliano sólo puede llenarse con la imagen.* (2: 1215)
>
> • • •
>
> since man is an image, he participates as such and in the end he comes upon the total clarification of the image; if the image were denied him he would have no knowledge at all of the resurrection. The image is the incessant complement of what is half-seen and what is half-heard, the fearful Pascalian *entredeux* can only be filled with the image.

The image, Lezama stresses, is not its own finality, it is the vehicle to achieve mystical union with God: "En realidad, todo soporte de la imagen es hipertélico, va más allá de su finalidad, la desconoce y ofrece la infinita sorpresa de lo que yo he llamado *éxtasis de participación en lo homogéneo*, un punto errante, una imagen, por la extensión" (2: 1215). ("Actually, every support of the image is hypertelic, goes beyond its finality, does not know it and offers the infinite surprise of what I have called the *ecstasy of participation in the homogeneous*, a shifting point, an image, by extension.") "Ecstasy of participation in the homogeneous" refers to the Nirvana-like state that also appears in Lezama's writings under the name *hypertelia* and is associated with the resurrection of the flesh proclaimed in the Apostles' Creed and the hesychastic rhythm achieved by José Cemí at the end of *Paradiso*. The way to reach this state of ecstasy is through excess, through a lack of restraint; the *desmesura* that characterizes Lezama's style is a microcosmic reflection of the excess, of the total plenitude of God:

> *Si la potencia actuase sin la imagen, sería tan solo un acto autodestructivo y sin participación, pero todo acto, toda potencia es un crecimiento infinito, una desmesura, en el que lo estelar apuntala lo telúrico. La imagen, al participar en el acto, entrega como una visibilidad momentánea, que sin ella, sin la imagen como único recurso al alcance del hombre, sería una desmesura impenetrable. De esa manera, el hombre se apodera de esa desmesura, la hace surgir y reincorpora una nueva desmesura. Toda poiesis es un acto de participación en esta desmesura, una participación del hombre en el espíritu universal, en el Espíritu Santo, en la madre universal. (2: 1216)*
>
> • • •
>
> If potency acted without the image, it would only be a self-destructive act without participation, but every act, every potency is an infinite growth, an excess, in which the stellar braces the telluric. The image, when it participates in the act, yields a sort of momentary visibility, without it, without the image as the only recourse within the reach of man, it would be an impenetrable excess. In this manner, man appropriates this excess, makes it surge up and reincorporates a new excess. All *poiesis* is an act of man's participation in this excess, a participation in the universal spirit, in the Holy Spirit, in the universal mother.

For Lezama the practice of poetry (which for him encompasses all reading as well as all writing) is both an allegory of the process of salvation through illumination and the actual process that leads to salvation. The time (and the space) Lezama seeks to create in his novels is, therefore, that of immortality.

Despite stylistic similarities that would suggest a kinship with postmodernist writers (Severo Sarduy, for example), Lezama's view of *poiesis* precludes his participation in their essentially nihilistic worldview. Lezama is undeniably fascinated by the richness of language, its ambiguities, its texture, its acoustic resonances (e.g., "minas de cartón y de carbón"). In his writing there is uninhibited pleasure, and his humor—sometimes childish but often capable of mordant satire—is a constant presence. Unlike Sarduy, however, Lezama does not profess a concept of artistic creation as play.

In "Confluencias" Lezama relates his first encounter with the image, a nocturnal hallucination of a hand that reached out to his own hand in the dark, and he asks a question that summarizes his ideological stance: "¿Convertir una experiencia decisiva y terrible en simple juego verbal, en literatura?" (2: 1210). ("To convert a decisive and terrible experience into a simple verbal game, into literature?") Without the image, *poiesis* for Lezama becomes an act of self-destruction.

Chapter 3
· · · · · · ·

The Ethics of Androgyny:
A Sexual Parable

*I saw many herds of naked souls who were all lamenting
most miserably, and different laws seemed to be laid on
them, some lying supine on the ground, some sitting all
crouched up, and some moving on continually; those
going about were the greatest number and those lying
in torment fewest but their tongues most loosed by
the pain.*
　　　—Dante, Inferno, *Canto 14 (trans. John D. Sinclair)*

*If the visit of an insect, that is to say the transportation
of the seed from another flower, is generally necessary for
the fertilisation of a flower, that is because self-
fertilisation, the insemination of a flower by itself, would
lead, like a succession of intermarriages in the same
family, to degeneracy and sterility . . .*
　　　—Marcel Proust, Cities of the Plain
　　(trans. C. K. Scott Moncrieff and Terence Kilmartin)

· · ·

L
ezama holds fast to the belief that the ultimate value of
metaphorical language does not lie in the delights of self-
referential word-play, but in the ability of the poetic image
to discover meaning. The torrential succession of signifiers that
characterizes his prose has as its goal not the production of provisional meanings, but the precipitation of a transcendental signified. Lezama, therefore, sees the circularity of self-referential postmodernist discourse as a tempting though deadly trap. In *Paradiso*,
through the symbolical treatment of sexual deviations, and homosexuality in particular, Lezama fashions a parable that warns of the
artistic and spiritual self-destruction inherent in a discourse that
turns in upon itself.

Once more, the stylistic similarities and the phantasmagoric portrayal of deviant sexual activity recall the favorite topoi of Severo
Sarduy, and it becomes necessary to underscore the different role
played by eroticism in the works of the two Cuban novelists. While
it is true that both Lezama and Sarduy conceive of the erotic in sex
and in language as *dépense*, as the cultivation of the superfluous, the
goal-less, for which the waste of the seed—whether as semen or

seme—is essential, the novelists diverge in their final appreciation of eroticism.[1] Although the erotic is embraced uninhibitedly in *Paradiso* as an important part of life and poetic experience, Lezama ultimately does not share Sarduy's conception of eroticism and erotic discourse as an end in itself.

Sexual deviations in Lezama's novel are represented as dead ends from which it is impossible to issue to the golden region of poetry, the space of Gnosis where creation, death, and resurrection can occur. The concept of the golden region is described in Chapter 9 as follows: ". . . la compenetración entre la fijeza estelar y las incesantes mutaciones de las profundidades marinas, contribuyen a formar una región dorada para un hombre que resiste todas las posibilidades del azar con una inmensa sabiduría placentera" (*Obras completas*, 1: 329) ("the interpenetration of the fixedness of the stars and the incessant mutations of the marine depths . . . form a gilded zone for a man who can resist all the possibilities of chance with an immense [joyful] wisdom" [*Paradiso*, trans. Rabassa, p. 233]). Since in Lezama's view ethics and aesthetics are inseparable, reaching this golden region is both a moral and an artistic goal for José Cemí. Throughout *Paradiso*, homosexuality, madness, and suicide appear as the most dangerous detours faced by Cemí in his years of poetic apprenticeship, and they are understood by Lezama as versions of the same danger, the loss of reason (*logos*).

Since the publication of *Paradiso* in 1966, the significance of homosexuality in the novel has elicited polemics in which both extraliterary and critical concerns have been addressed.[2] Rodríguez Monegal, for instance, rejects the view that *Paradiso* is an apology for homosexuality disguised as a novel in the manner of Gide's *Corydon*. Although he correctly stresses the basic formal and ideological differences between *Paradiso* and *Corydon*, I believe that the dialogues on homosexuality in Chapters 9 and 10 of *Paradiso*, where, in fact, *Corydon* is mentioned (1: 429), owe much to Gide's tract. As in *Corydon*, the discussion is motivated by a scandal, and zoological, philosophical, historical and moral arguments are employed.

Despite the notoriety gained by the role of homosexuality in *Paradiso*, the curious connection made in the novel between madness and homosexuality has yet to be examined in the context of Lezama's philosophical system. This is the problem I will attempt to elucidate.

Enrique Lihn's "*Paradiso*, novela y homosexualidad" argues convincingly for the ambivalent horror and fascination that the "sin contra natura" exerts on "the chaste and innocuous voyeur Cemí" and Lezama himself.[3] Ambivalence notwithstanding, Lihn correctly perceives that Lezama assigns a negative value to homosexuality in the novel—"the *evaluational discourse* of *Paradiso* . . . and the plot (Foción's fate among others) condemn and punish homosexuality, they perhaps attempt to exorcize it, they oppose to it 'a category superior to sex,' Cemí's perfect and creative androgyny"[4]—and sees the hesychastic rhythm achieved in the realm of androgyny by the young artist at the conclusion of the novel as an antidote to homosexuality.[5]

It is now generally accepted that José Cemí, Ricardo Fronesis, and Eugenio Foción, besides being metaphors that became characters (as Lezama has explained) are indeed aspects of one personality.[6] Thus in this triad of friendship, Fronesis, whose name in Greek, *phronesis*, meaning "prudence," alludes to the prime virtue of the Stoics,[7] represents order, a life guided by a *telos*, heterosexual intercourse, and an expansive or diastaltic style. Although some critics of *Paradiso* identify the character Fronesis with wisdom, it is necessary to stress the Stoic definition of the word *phronesis* as "prudence," since Lezama himself emphasizes Fronesis's Stoic characteristics from his first appearance in the novel: "Fronesis mostraba siempre, junto con una alegría que brotaba de su salud espiritual, una dignidad estoica, que parecía alejarse de las cosas para obtener, paradojalmente, su inefable simpatía" (1: 303). ("Fronesis always showed, along with the good cheer that [flowed] from his spiritual health, a stoical dignity, which seemed to withdraw from things, paradoxically, in order to achieve [their] ineffable charm" [p. 215].)

The relationship between Cemí and Fronesis is thus ruled by the Stoic concept of *sympathos*, whereas for Foción Cemí clearly experiences the opposite: "Las leyes del *apathos* de los estoicos funcionaron de inmediato, no, no le cayó nada bien Foción a Cemí" (1: 319). ("The Stoics' idea of apathy went to work immediately; no, Foción did not make a good impression on Cemí at all" [p. 226].) The Stoic definition also permits a distinction between *phronesis* and *sophia* that is important in distinguishing the roles of Fronesis and Cemí. *Sophia* (wisdom) will be the province of "el viejo sabio niño" ("the old wise child"), Cemí; *phronesis* (practical wisdom, according to Aristotle), that of his friend. Foción, in turn, embodies chaos, a life without a *telos*, homosexual intercourse, and a contracting or systaltic style. José Cemí, as we have already seen, incorporates the essential aspects of Foción and Fronesis, chaos and order, in a life guided by hypertelia[8] and androgyny and characterized by an appeasing or hesychastic style.

The diastaltic, systaltic, and hesychastic styles are the three keys of ancient Greek harmony. *The Oxford English Dictionary* gives the following definitions: *diastaltic*, "Applied to a style of melody fitted to expand or exalt the mind"; *systaltic*, "Applied to a style of melody having the effect of, contracting, or depressing the mind"; *hesychastic*, "Applied to a style of melody which tends to appease the mind." Lezama never mentions the *diastaltic* style, but his characterization of Fronesis fully warrants the association I suggest. The following explanation of the traditional use of these keys is particularly relevant to our discussion of Lezama's ethics:

> The diastaltic ethos of musical composition is that which expresses grandeur and manly elevation of soul, and heroic actions; and these are employed in tragedy and all poetry that approaches the tragic type. The systaltic ethos is that by which the soul is brought down into a humble and unmanly frame; and such a disposition will be fitting for amatory effusions and dirges and lamentations and the like. And the hesychastic or tranquilly disposed ethos of musical composition is that which is followed by calmness of soul and a liberal and peaceful disposition: and this temper will fit hymns, paeans, laudations, didactic poetry and the like.[9]

I believe that the three friends are also emblematized by the figurines Foción habitually describes when someone visits his room: the bronze statuette of Narcissus (Foción), the flute player on a Greek vase (Fronesis), and a statuette of Lao-tse, "the old wise child" riding a buffalo (Cemí). Foción defines or characterizes the three objects in the following manner:

> . . . señalaba el Narciso y decía: "La imagen de la imagen, la nada." Señalaba el aprendizaje del adolescente griego, y decía: "El deseo que conoce, el conocimiento por el hilo continuo del sonido de los infiernos." Parecía después que le daba una pequeña palmada en las ancas del búfalo montado por Lao-tse y decía: "El huevo empolla en el espacio vacío." (1: 410–411)
>
> • • •
>
> Foción would point to the Narcissus and say, "The image of the image, nothingness." He would point to the apprenticeship of the Greek adolescent and say, "The desire that knows, knowledge through the continuous thread of the sound of hell." Then he would give a small pat to the rump of Lao-tse's buffalo, and say, "The egg hatches in empty space." (p. 292)

Significantly only Lao-tse, who symbolizes Cemí, survives the fury of the red-haired boy: "Dentro del cuarto de Foción, el búfalo, tri-

pulado por el maestro del vacío del cielo silencioso, se sintió de
nuevo dueño de la montaña y del lago y del oeste, impulsado por el
sonido de las colgadas placas de nefrita, la piedra sonora" (1: 415).
("Inside Foción's room, the buffalo, ridden by the master of the void
[of] the silent heaven, once more perceived himself lord of the mountain and the lake and the west, goaded on by the sound of dangling
plates of [nephrite,] the sonorous stone" [p. 295].) The sound of the
nephrite chimes seems to be an allusion to the hesychastic rhythm,
the rhythm of androgyny and poetic self-sufficiency. This chiming is
akin to the sound of the spoon stirring a glass of coffee which precipitates Cemí's *moment privilégié* and final conversion to poetry at
the very end of the novel:

> Comenzó a golpear con la cucharilla en el vaso, agitando lentamente
> su contenido. Impulsado por el tintineo, Cemí corporizó de nuevo
> a Oppiano Licario. Las sílabas que oía eran ahora más lentas, pero
> también más claras y evidentes. Era la misma voz, pero modulada en
> otro registro. Volvía a oír de nuevo: ritmo hesicástico, podemos em-
> pezar. (1: 645)
>
> . . .
>
> [He began to strike the glass with the spoon, slowly stirring its contents.
> Impelled by the ringing, Cemí once more gave body to Oppiano Licario.
> The syllables he heard were now slower, but also clearer and more evi-
> dent. It was the same voice, but modulated in another register. Once
> more he heard: hesychastic rhythm, we can begin.]

The leading example of madness in *Paradiso* is Foción, whose deviant *eros* (particularly his frustrated desire for Fronesis) leads to the
loss of his reason (*logos*). Cemí witnesses the mental crisis precipitated by Foción's realization that the mother of the red-haired boy
has been encouraging their homosexual relationship in order to de-
flect her son's incestuous advances. Foción's bitter remarks to Cemí
are punctuated by the laughter of impending insanity:

> Me rogó que buscara a su hijo, no que lo tolerase cuando huía de su
> rechazo. Le parecía normal que su hijo se abandonase al Eros de los
> griegos, con tal de que no fuera monstruosamente incestuoso. Lo único
> que hace siempre al homosexualismo, ja, ja, ja, ja, já, es evitar un mal
> mayor, en mi caso, ja, já, no me he suicidado, pero creo que me he
> vuelto loco, ja, ja, já—. (1: 495)
>
> . . .
>
> She begged me to search for her son, not just to tolerate him when he
> fled her rejection. It seemed normal to her that her son should abandon

himself to the Eros of the Greeks so long as he wasn't monstrously incestuous. The one thing that homosexuality always achieves, ha, ha, ha, ha, ha, is to avoid a greater evil, in my case, ha, ha, I didn't commit suicide, instead I think I've gone crazy, ha, ha, ha. (p. 354)

The meeting of Foción and Cemí in the café at this crucial moment represents a confrontation of ideologies. Suicide, homosexuality, and madness, the three alternatives Foción perceives as his lot in life, are opposed to Cemí's heterodox Catholicism, which sees poetic epiphany as the means to salvation and resurrection. The series of alternatives presented or implied in this episode recall the three choices that according to André Gide are available to modern man: suicide, homosexuality, or Catholicism.

Lezama not only fuses his concept of Catholicism with poetic revelation, but following Dante associates homosexuality with violence done to art. The essay "Plenitud relacionable" ("Relational Plenitude"), a characteristic death-defying leap, in which Lezama attempts to metaphorize the essential philosophical stance of Dante, Gide, and Claudel, explicitly makes this link between homosexuality and violence toward art:

El más paseador y sombrío de los gibelinos [Dante] pareció prefigurar arduas relaciones contemporáneas. En el séptimo círculo, recinto tercero, puesto a la moda por ciertas indiscreciones de Gide [Corydon], los violentos contra la naturaleza aparecen nivelados con los violentos contra el arte. (2: 475)

· · ·

The best traveled and somber of the Ghibellines [Dante] seems to have prefigured arduous contemporary relations. In the seventh circle, third round, made fashionable by certain indiscretions of Gide [*Corydon*], the violent against nature appear as the equals of the violent against art.

In order to understand the allusion to Dante and its particular importance to Lezama it is necessary to review the passage in question. John D. Sinclair's commentary on this canto of the *Inferno* allows us to follow Lezama's formulation:

In accordance with the plan of the lower Hell outlined in the eleventh canto the sins punished in the third round of the seventh circle, on the burning plain, are: violence directly against God—blasphemy, violence against nature, God's child—sodomy, and violence against art or industry, 'to God, as it were, a grandchild'—usury; and the first idea we get of the whole round is that of *barrenness*, it is 'a plain that rejects every

plant from its bed'. The blasphemers who confronted God in their inso-
lence now confront Him forever in their agony; the sodomites are driven
about by the unrest of their old, corrupt passion; the usurers crouch
permanently over their money-bags; and such sins leave the soul sterile.
These sins, in one way or other directed specifically against the divine
ordering of human life, are all regarded as in a peculiar sense sins
against God, so that they are punished by that which is the special symbol of God's anger, such a 'fire from the Lord out of heaven' as destroyed
Sodom and Gomorrah.[10]

The sterility and the circular restlessness of homosexuals in Dante
are adopted by Lezama. The fire from heaven becomes "lightning,"
the thunderbolt of Zeus, in the cases of Godofredo and Foción, but
also retains its Biblical connotation of brimstone. Lezama, however,
does not adopt the definition of art as "industry" and violence as
"usury" but uses "art" in the modern sense. The fact that blasphemy, sodomy, and sins against art are all considered sins against
God is vital for the ethics of Lezama.

The essay "Plenitud relacionable" is ultimately an attack on the
contemporary "self-destructive fervor" that Lezama sees as frivolous and superfluous. Addressing Mallarmé, Valéry, and Gide, he rejects the concept of randomness, and, siding with Claudel, concludes: "el católico sabe que ninguno de sus actos es inconsecuente,
tiene gratuidad, sino que aun en la revelación tiene composición"
(2: 479) ("a Catholic knows that none of his acts is inconsequential,
gratuitous, but that even in revelation it has design"). This *gra-
tuitousness* rejected by Lezama is also that of Gide's Corydon, who
uses his characterization of sexuality as "luxury" and "gratuitous-
ness" to refute the view that homosexuality is "against nature."[11]

After the incident at the café, when Cemí next sees his friend,
Foción is in the ward for mental patients at the same hospital where
Augusta, Cemí's grandmother, is dying:

*Al lado del álamo, en el jardín del pabellón de los desrazonados, vio un
hombre joven con su uniforme blanco, describiendo incesantes círculos
alrededor del álamo agrandado por una raíz cuidada. Era Foción.
Volvía en sus círculos una y otra vez como si el álamo fuera su Dios y
su destino.* (1: 518)

· · ·

Beside the poplar, in the mental ward's garden, he saw a young man in a
white uniform describing circles incessantly around the poplar, whose
size was owed to its well-tended roots. It was Foción. He went round

and round in his circles, as if the poplar were his God and his destiny. (p. 371)

Cemí has no difficulty interpreting Foción's inexorable circling of the tree. The poplar is Fronesis, who is both Foción's God (*logos* in the sense used by the gospel of St. John) and destination (*telos*): "Cemí supo de súbito que el árbol para Foción, regado por sus incesantes y enloquecidos paseos circulares, era Fronesis" (1: 519) (Cemí suddenly realized that to Foción, the tree irrigated by his incessant, maddened rounds was Fronesis" [p. 371]).[12] Cemí's grandmother dies the next day, having opened her eyes for the last time the previous night during an electric storm. During that storm the poplar is struck by lightning, and Cemí discovers, after his grandmother expires, that Foción is gone: "El rayo que había destruido el árbol había liberado a Foción de la adoración de su eternidad circular" (1: 520) ("The lightning that had destroyed the tree had freed Foción from his adoration of circular eternity" [p. 372]). The revelation of Foción's fate and liberation acquires the nature of a warning for Cemí, particularly in the context of his last conversation with Augusta. This conversation re-enacts the famous scene of Chapter 9 in which Cemí's mother consecrates him to the poetic search that will earn him salvation and differentiates between the danger undertaken by the sick, a danger without epiphany, and the necessary danger that will lead to transfiguration (1: 320–322). On her deathbed, Augusta approvingly marks Cemí's progress, and contrasts his gift for observing "ese ritmo que hace el cumplimiento, el cumplimiento de lo que desconocemos, pero que, como tú dices, nos ha sido dictado como el signo principal de nuestro vivir" (1: 518) ("the rhythm that makes a [fulfilment, the fulfilment of what we do not know,] but which, as you say, has been dictated to us as the principal mark of our lives" [p. 371]), with the sterility of persons who disrupt, "favorecen el vacío" (1: 517) ["favor the void"], persons like Foción.

The association of madness with sexual deviance and ceaseless circular movement drawn by Foción's fate is both prefigured and repeated in other episodes, but nowhere with the richness of symbolism found in the story of Godofredo el Diablo told by Fronesis to Cemí at the end of Chapter 8.[13] As in the case of the passage that we have just examined, the story itself gains in significance from the context in which it is told, Cemí's first private conversation with Fronesis. The story of Godofredo's loss of reason comes to complete the triad, filling the future place of Foción, whom Cemí has not yet met. Godofredo's beauty is immediately described as being domi-

nated by a fury similar to that of the Tibetan bear, also known as the
Chinese demon, "que describe incesantes círculos, como si se fuera
a morder a sí mismo" (1: 302) ["that incessantly describes circles,
as if it were going to bite itself"]. This fury already foreshadows
Foción's Dantesque circling of the poplar.

Godofredo's sexual deviance (voyeurism) and his madness, in turn,
reflect those of Father Eufrasio whose study of concupiscence in St.
Paul, "la cópula sin placer, le había tomado todo el tuétano, doble-
gándole la razón" (1:305) ("copulation without pleasure had sucked
the marrow out of him, putting his reason out of kilter" [p. 217]).
The priest's sexual obsession, "Cómo lograr en el encuentro amo-
roso la lejanía del otro cuerpo y cómo extraer el salto de la energía
suprema del gemido del dolor más que de toda inefabilidad placentera, le daban vueltas como un torniquete que se anillase en el es-
pacio, rodeado de grandes vultúridos" (1: 305) ("How to keep the
other body at a distance in an amorous encounter and still attain the
leap of supreme energy [from] the moan of pain [more than from any
pleasurable ineffability,] was plaguing him like a [tourniquet] spin-
ning in a space ringed by great vultures" [p. 217]), is also described by
a circular movement, the turning of the tourniquet which is both
the symbol of his madness and the prosaic instrument of his deviant
eroticism.

Godofredo secretly observes Father Eufrasio exercising his mania
with Fileba, and causes her husband's suicide by making him witness
the act. While fleeing from the dreadful results of his voyeuristic in-
trigues, Godofredo is blinded in one eye by one of the snake-like
vines, "se curvaban como serpientes verticalizadas" ("coiling like
rearing serpents"), which we are told, "le hizo justicia mayor, retro-
cedió, tomó impulso y le grabó una cruz en el ojo derecho, en el ojo
del canon" (1: 309) ("took its vengeance on him, and drawing back, it
drove forward and engraved a cross on his right eye, the canon
eye" [p. 219]). It is then that the red-haired Godofredo also loses his
reason: "Sus caminatas describen inmensos círculos indetenibles,
cuyos radios zigzaguean como la descarga de un rayo" (1: 309) ("His
walks describe immense, implacable circles, with the radii zigzag-
ging like bolts of lightning" [p. 219]).

This story of punished voyeurism, which seems to be a warning directed at the innocuous voyeur, Cemí, contains all the topoi
that Lezama links to sexual deviance. The deviant eroticism of
Godofredo and Father Eufrasio is linked to their madness and to the
suicide of Fileba's husband. Godofredo's circular walks, the image of
the thunderbolt, and Godofredo's red hair, which foreshadows that
of the incestuous red-haired boy, all forecast the episode of Foción's

madness. The three alternatives Foción outlines in the café—suicide, homosexuality (here, deviant eroticism in general), and madness—are, therefore, already present in the story of Godofredo, although dispersed among several characters.

Upon closer examination the allusion to the canonical eye in the story of Godofredo, which on the surface appears to be an irrelevant digression, reveals another important nexus. The significance of the "canonical eye" is partially explained in the story itself:

> *El ojo de nublo era el derecho, el que los teólogos llaman el ojo del canon, pues al que le faltaba no podía leer los libros sagrados en el sacrificio. El que no tuviese ese ojo jamás podría ser sacerdote. Parecía como si inconscientemente Godofredo supiese el valor intrínseco que los cánones le dan a ese ojo, pues se contentaba con ser Godofredo el Diablo.* (1: 302)
>
> . . .
>
> The foggy eye was the right one, the one theologians call the canon eye, for a person who lacks it cannot read the sacred book during the elevation, and thus could never be a priest. It was as if Godofredo unconsciously knew the intrinsic value that the canons gave to that eye of his, for he was content to be Godofredo the Devil. (p. 214)

Beyond the fact that the loss of his eye makes him an outcast and leads him to opt for evil, there is an additional sexual significance to Godofredo's blinding. Since he is a voyeur, his eye can be considered to be his sexual organ and his blinding may be seen as a symbolical castration. The sexual meaning of the loss of the canonical eye is reinforced when we recall that canon law traditionally proscribed a man who "caret aliqua membrorum" ["lacks any member"] from holy orders.[14]

In *Paradiso*, as discussed below, homosexuality is associated with castration, blindness, and exclusion from the "priesthood" that leads to poetry and salvation. This exclusion of homosexuals and eunuchs from Paradise and/or Resurrection, based on St. Thomas Aquinas's characterization of homosexuality as a sin of bestiality rather than lust, is discussed by Cemí in his answer to Foción's defense of homosexuality in Chapter 9:

> Los vicios contra natura no son los pecados más graves entre los pecados de la lujuria, *vuelve a decir, parece que el aquinatense considere la lujuria como una equivocación de la semilla en la germinación, pecado grosero de exceso, pues poco más adelante, en la* Suma *nos dice:* El adulterio, el estupro, el rapto, el sacrilegio, contrarían más la caridad del

prójimo que el acto contra natura, *parece, si nos apresuramos un poco,*
que reconoce una aridez demoníaca, una semilla yerta sembrada en la
noche perniciosa. Pero, al fin, Santo Tomás dice, después de un largo
rodeo, lo que tiene que decir refiriéndose al pecado contra natura; no se
contiene bajo la malicia, sino bajo la bestialidad. (1: 376–377)

• • •

'Sins against nature are not the gravest sins among the sins of lust,' he
says again. It seems that Aquinas considers lust an error of the genera-
tive seed, a sin of gross excess; a little farther on in the *Summa* he tells
us that 'adultery, rape, elopement, sacrilege would be more harmful to
the charity of one's neighbor than an act against nature.' He seems to
recognize a demoniacal aridity, a frigid seed sown in the pernicious
night. But in the end, after much circumlocution, St. Thomas says what
he has to say about the sin against nature: 'It is not classified under
malice but under bestiality.' (p. 268)

Again, in Cemí's interpretation of Aquinas, sterility becomes the
major objection to homosexuality. Godofredo's tale, therefore, incorporates all the major potential dangers which Cemí must overcome
in order to achieve artistic fertility, the hesychastic rhythm.

The endless circling of Foción, Godofredo el Diablo, and Father
Eufrasio and the snake-like vine that pierces Godofredo's eye recall
one of Lezama's favorite topoi, the *ouroboros*, the snake that swallows its own tail. In fact, the first description of Godofredo as a Tibetan bear contains an allusion to the *ouroboros:* "como si se fuera a
morder a sí mismo" (1: 302) ["as if it were going to bite itself"]. In
the context of Lezama's novel, the *ouroboros* signifies both the "sin
against nature" and its punishment. Foción's etymological games
with the name of Anubis (the jackalheaded god who conducts the
dead in the Egyptian underworld) shortly before losing his reason
reveal both the meaning of Godofredo's blind eye and the particular meaning Lezama attaches to the *ouroboros.* Foción describes the
anus as the eye of Anubis by playing on the pun *ano/Anubis* (anus/
Anubis). He then characterizes it as a blind eye, and sodomy as "la
anía [pun on *ano* (anus) and *manía* (mania)] del dios Anubis, que
quiere guiar donde no hay caminos, que ofrece lo alto del cuerpo in-
ferior, el ano, el anillo de Saturno, en el valle de los muertos" (1: 492)
("the [ania] of the God Anubis, who wants to [lead] where there are
no paths, who offers the high part of the lower body, the anus, the
[ring] of Saturn, in the valley of the dead") (p. 352). Sodomy, then,
recreates the symbolic gesture of the *ouroboros;* "el serpentín intestinal" (1: 343) ("intestinal snake" [p. 244]) described in the Leregas–
Baena Albornoz episode of Chapter 9 swallows "la serpiente fálica"

(1: 493) ("the phallic serpent" [p. 353]) of the gods who accompany
Anubis in Chapter 11.

In order to transcend the merely physical analogy between homosexuality and the *ouroboros* and understand the new philosophical significance that Lezama attaches to this ancient symbol, we
must first note two relevant stages in its genealogy: its meaning in
Gnostic systems and in alchemy. In the Gnostic systems, the snake
had the opposite symbolism to what it has in the Judeo-Christian
system: "Gnostic snake worshippers, the Ophites . . . radically re-
interpreted Genesis. In their view the snake was divine because he
wanted to enlighten mankind with the knowledge of good and evil
and give them eternal life, while God . . . wished to keep men earth-
bound and ignorant."[15] From this snake of the Ophites, giver of eternal life and knowledge, we go to the *ouroboros* as interpreted by alchemists. The tail-eating serpent "has no beginning and no end; it
devours itself and renews itself. Life and death, creation and destruction, are an unending circular process; out of the one comes the
other."[16] In their imagery, alchemists, unlike the Ophites, dwell
both on the positive and negative aspects of serpents: "Serpents (or
toads and dragons, which have the same associations) represent base
matter, which must be 'killed.' They are 'venomous' and 'evil,' but
at the same time carry the Philosopher's stone within."[17] The goal of
all alchemists is to find the Philosopher's stone and extract it from
base matter. Thus for the alchemists the *ouroboros* is a symbol of
the eternal cycle of life and death.

Michael Maier's *Atalanta Fugiens*, published in 1618, gives an alchemical variation of the *ouroboros*.[18] In this case the cycle of life
and death is represented by a woman nursing a poisonous toad. She
then sickens and dies so that the toad, who is seen as her child, may
live. This emblem leads us back to *Paradiso*, where Foción enlists a
similar scenario in order to urge the acceptance of homosexuality:

*Cuando Electra creyó que había parido un dragón, vio que el monstruo
lloraba porque quería ser lactado; sin vacilaciones le da su pecho, sa-
liendo después la leche mezclada con la sangre. Aunque había parido
un monstruo, cosa que tendría que desconcertarla, sabía que su respuesta tenía que ser no dejarlo morir de hambre, pues la grandeza del
hombre consiste en que puede asimilar lo que le es desconocido.* (1: 348)

• • •

When Electra thought she'd given birth to a dragon, she saw that the
monster was crying to be nursed; she gives it her breast without hesita-
tion and the milk comes out mixed with blood. Even though she had
given birth to a monster, something which must have disconcerted her,

she knew that her response had to be to keep it from dying of hunger, because the greatness of man consists in his ability to assimilate what's unknown to him. (p. 247)

Foción's literary allusion (or Lezama's) has been radically altered both in content and in interpretation to suit the needs of the moment. It is Clytemnestra who in Aeschylus's *The Libation Bearers* dreams that she gives birth to a snake, suckles it, and is horrified when it draws blood with the milk. Orestes, told about the dream, interprets it as a prophecy:

> But I pray to the earth and to my father's grave that this dream is for me and that I will succeed. See, I divine it, and it coheres all in one piece. If this snake came out of the same place whence I came, if she wrapped it in robes, as she wrapped me, and if its jaws gaped wide around the breast that suckled me, and if it stained the intimate milk with an outburst of blood, so that for fright and pain she cried aloud, it follows then, that as she nursed this hideous thing of prophecy, she must be cruelly murdered. I turn snake to kill her. This is what the dream portends.[19]

For Aeschylus the nursing snake is a symbol of the horror of matricide, symbolized by the unnatural commingling of the milk and the blood, whereas for Foción the nursing dragon signifies the greatness of the human race, its ability to assimilate the unknown. The symbolism attached by Foción to the dragon is diametrically opposed to the role played by the dragon in Cemí's (and Lezama's) conception of artistic creation as it is suggested in the description of Rialta's fibroma at the end of Chapter 10, where the dangerous proliferation of the cells becomes an emblem of Lezama's own style. Foción associates the dragon with homosexuality, but for Lezama all sex *contra natura* falls principally under the aegis of the *ouroboros*.

Within Lezama's system of imagery, therefore, the tail-eating snake is not seen as the ultimate symbol of the creative process, since the eternal cycle of life and destruction posited by the *ouroboros* (a concept borrowed by the alchemists from the Stoic doctrine of the conflagration) is essentially inimical to Lezama's fundamental, if heterodox, Christianity.[20] The progress of the poet in life must, like Christian history, have a moment of rupture like the *Parousia*; it must reach a stage of transfiguration. This is why for Cemí and Lezama, the *ouroboros*, which is *atelic* (goal-less), is also *atelos* (incomplete, imperfect) and must be destroyed, not so that it can return in the same form, but rather in order to precipitate a necessary metamorphosis. The snake must be transfigured into a hybrid, the dragon, which here becomes the symbol of hypertelia, of resurrection. This endows the passage, discussed in Chapter 2 in terms of the author's aesthetics, with a religious significance:

> *en los cuerpos que logra la imaginación, hay que destruir el elemento serpiente para dar paso al elemento dragón, un organismo que está hecho para devorarse en el círculo, tiene que destruirse para que irrumpa una nueva bestia, surgiendo del lago sulfúrico, pidiéndole prestadas sus garras a los grandes vultúridos y su cráneo al can tricéfalo que cuida las moradas subterráneas.* (1: 453)
>
> . . .
>
> [in the bodies achieved by imagination, it is necessary to destroy the serpent element to make way for the dragon element, an organism which is made to devour itself in the circle has to destroy itself so that a new beast can take over, emerging from the sulphuric lake, borrowing its claws from the great vultures and its craneum from the three-headed dog that guards the subterranean dwellings.]

To the contracting or systaltic rhythm of homosexuality, symbolized by the *ouroboros*, Lezama opposes the tranquillity of the hesychastic rhythm of androgyny, the dragon. Unlike the snake of the *ouroboros*, Lezama's dragon is a composite creature born of human imagination and as such is part of the major goal of poetry: the re-creation of nature after the fall. This all-encompassing rhythm is the goal of Cemí's poetic apprenticeship, and at the end of Chapter 13, Oppiano Licario verifies Cemí's achievement: "Veo . . . que ha pasado del estilo sistáltico, o de las pasiones tumultuosas, al estilo hesicástico, o del equilibrio anímico, en muy breve tiempo . . . Entonces, podemos ya empezar" (1: 589). ["I see . . . that you have passed from the systaltic style, that of tumultuous passions, to the hesychastic style, that of spiritual equilibrium, in a very brief time. . . . Then, we can already begin"]. In Chapter 14, these very words close and at the same time open the conclusion of *Paradiso*, "ritmo hesicástico, podemos empezar" (1: 645)["hesychastic rhythm, we can begin"].

As we have seen, for Lezama, madness, the loss of reason (the *logos*) is equated with the loss or waste of the *logos spermatikos* (seminal reason) in homosexuality. Lezama repeatedly associates homosexuality with the waste of the seed, sterility, and castration. Probably, the clearest example is his description of Leregas's sexual preference, "su Eros de gratuidad" ["his gratuitous Eros"] as "el fuego del nacimiento malo, de la esperma derramada sobre el azufre incandescente" (1: 342) ["the fire of bad birth, of sperm spilled over incandescent brimstone"], and although we know from his exhibitionistic adventures in Chapter 8 that Leregas is a "coloso fálico" (1: 278) ("phallic colossus" [p. 198]), after his intercourse with Baena he is described as an "eunuco poseedor" (1: 344) ("possessing eunuch") (p. 244). The sterile circularity of the *ouroboros* reflects the waste of the seed in all sex *contra natura*. Those who lose their *logos* (direction) are condemned to wander incessantly in Luciferine circles like Godofredo el Diablo, Foción, and even Fronesis's real mother, who likewise suffers from a sexual psychosis, "en forma de dromomanía mitomaníaca, caminaba, caminaba y bailaba por las noches de Viena, en seguimiento de dólmenes viriles" (1: 399) ("in a form of mythomaniacal dromomania; at night in Vienna she used to walk and walk and dance in pursuit of virile dolmens" [p. 284]).[21]

To this endless and destructive wandering Lezama opposes Fronesis's *telos* and order. The configuration of the opposition between Fronesis and Foción represents the equilibrium that will permit Cemí to reach the all-encompassing state of androgyny. Though he is stricken like Foción by the fear of the "vagina dentada" (1: 447) ("toothed vagina" [p. 319]), Fronesis utilizes the *ouroboros* in the form of a circle of cloth cut from his undershirt as an antidote to overcome his fear of Lucía's "delicioso enemigo" (1:403) ("delicious enemy" [p. 287]). Fronesis explains this crucial experience to Cemí:

> —Mira, el día que yo no pude ir a la cita con Foción y contigo, tenía que verme con Lucía, me pasó, cierto que tan solo un instante, lo mismo que a Foción. Pero hice en la camiseta un agujero que tapaba el resto del sexo de Lucía, que se escondía detrás del círculo protector. Había un misterio mayor, a él acudí y creo que eso me salvó. (1: 448–449)
>
> • • •
>
> "Look, the day I couldn't keep the date with Foción and you, I had to see Lucía; just for an instant, of course, the same thing that happened to Foción happened to me. But I made a hole in my undershirt that covered the rest of Lucía's sex, which was hidden behind the protective circle. There was a greater mystery, I came to it, and I think that saved me."
> (p. 320)

When he throws the undershirt into the sea Fronesis symbolically rejects the *ouroboros* and the view of existence that it represents. In terms of the geometrical allegory offered by his peculiar coitus with Lucía, the straight line of Christian history pierces (transcends) the deceitful circle of homosexuality: "La camiseta . . . se fue circulizando como una serpiente a la que alguien ha transmitido la inmortalidad" (1: 417) ("the undershirt coiled itself like a snake on which someone has conferred immortality" [p. 297]).[22]

Heterosexual coitus is seen as a loss of immortality, but that very loss is the source of creativity: "era necesario crear al perder precisamente la inmortalidad. Así el hombre fue mortal, pero creador, y la serpiente fálica se convirtió en un fragmento que debe resurgir" (1: 417) ("it was necessary to create precisely in order to lose immortality. Thus man was mortal, but creator, and the phallic serpent became a fragment that [has] to rise again" [p. 297]). Once more that fragment is the dragon of hypertelia. Coitus between man and woman ends the paradise of childhood and re-enacts the fall of Adam and Eve in Eden, but the *felix culpa* must be repeated. Paradoxically, mortality must (as in Christianity) be embraced in order for creation and a true hypertelia of immortality (resurrection) to be possible.

Chapter 9 gives two rival interpretations of the term "la hipertelia de la inmortalidad" ["the hypertelia of immortality"]. Foción, who actually coins the phrase, identifies it with homosexuality:

Todo lo que hoy nos parece desvío sexual, surge en una reminiscencia, o en algo que yo me atrevería a llamar, sin temor a ninguna pedantería, una hipertelia de la inmortalidad, o sea una busca de la creación, de la sucesión de la criatura, más allá de toda causalidad de la sangre y aun del espíritu, la creación de algo hecho por el hombre, totalmente desconocido aun por la especie. (1: 351)

· · ·

Everything that we consider sexual deviation today rises up in a reminiscence, or in something that with no fear of being pedantic I call a hypertely of immortality, a search for creation, for a succession of the creature beyond all causality of blood and even of spirit, the creation of something made by man as yet completely unknown to the species. (p. 249–250)

Cemí corrects him, bringing the discussion to the privileged ground of Christian theology. He redefines the "hypertelia of immortality" as "la resurrección de los cuerpos" (1: 378) ["the resurrection of the flesh"], and characterizes homosexuality as a "falsa inocencia" (1: 372) ("false innocence") (p. 264).[23]

Like the snake of the Gnostic Ophites, homosexuality and other sexual deviations offer Cemí the knowledge of good and evil and a form of immortality which is understood as an eternal cycle of destruction and creation. Cemí sees this type of immortality as a false *telos* whose true nature is revealed in the *dromomania*, the ceaseless wandering of all the sexual psychotics in the novel. The immortality Foción preaches is precisely the type of danger without epiphany exposed by Rialta to her son Cemí. Foción's way is well represented by the circle of the *ouroboros* and by the statuette of Narcissus which he describes as "La imagen de la imagen, la nada" (1: 410) ("The image of the image, nothingness") (p. 292).

By means of his triple protagonist, Lezama gives not one but three portraits of the artist as a young man. The goal-less Foción is the portrait of a failed artist, overcome by darkness. In Fronesis, Lezama depicts the opposite: a young man who will perhaps not go beyond an earthly *telos* because of an excess of light. Cemí is Lezama's attempt to surpass this dichotomy and to resolve it in an equilibrium which will put an end to all passion and all striving. This is why Cemí is guided not by a *telos* but a *hypertelos*. He rejects the goal of immortality, but by accepting death he hopes to achieve a form of it through resurrection. Cemí will not wrest immortality through Luciferine pride or through the light of reason, but will yield to the "fijeza" ["fixedness"] of the hesychastic rhythm and the self-sufficient immobility of androgyny. In this sense the José Cemí of *Paradiso* is as much a repository of José Lezama Lima's dreams as he is a self-portrait.[24]

Chapter 4

Culture as Nature: An American Practice of Reading and Writing

*Do not all the achievements of a poet's predecessors and
contemporaries rightfully belong to him? Why should he
shrink from picking flowers where he finds them? Only
by making the riches of the others our own do we bring
anything great into being.*
              —Goethe, Gedenkausgabe

*What happens when a new work of art is created is
something that happens simultaneously to all the works
of art which preceded it. The existing monuments form
an ideal order among themselves, which is modified by
the introduction of the new (the really new) work of art
among them. The existing order is complete before
the new work arrives; for order to persist after the
supervention of novelty, the* whole *existing order must
be, if ever so slightly, altered; and so the relations,
proportions, values of each work of art toward the whole
are readjusted; and this is conformity between the old
and the new. Whoever has approved this idea of order, of
the form of European, of English literature will not find
it preposterous that the past should be altered by the
present as much as the present is directed by the past.*
      —T. S. Eliot, "Tradition and the Individual Talent"

*Tout texte se construit comme mosaïque de citations,
tout texte est absorption et transformation d'un autre
texte. A la place de la notion d'intersubjectivité s'installe
celle d'intertextualité, et le langage poétique se lit,
au moins, comme* double. *(Every text is constructed as
a mosaic of citations, every text is absorption and
transformation of another text. The idea of intersubjectivity is replaced by that of intertextuality, and
poetic language is read, at least, as* double.*)*
                  —Julia Kristeva, Semiotikè

*But actually there is no choice between historical and
hidden meaning; both are present. The figural structure
preserves the historical event while interpreting it as
revelation; and must preserve it in order to interpret it.*
              —Erich Auerbach, "Figura"

· · ·

Lezama's writing is all of a piece. His poetry, novels, tales, and what one hesitates to call his critical writings, all are written in the metaphorical, vertiginously allusive style that is consistent with his faith in the paradoxical illuminating power of hermeticism. Critics generally accept Lezama's claim that he evolved a poetic system, and attempts have been made to codify his terminology.[1] Any such codification, however, is rendered difficult (if not ultimately impossible) because there is much more poetic insight than critical systematization in Lezama's literary system. In this sense, the Cuban writer cannot be compared to European writers like Proust and Joyce who have consistent critical frameworks to which their work can be reduced by critics. It is impossible to imagine a book about Lezama akin to J. P. Dalton's and C. Hart's *A Skeleton Key to "Finnegans Wake."* There is no "skeleton key" to *Paradiso* or to *Oppiano Licario;* they unconditionally require new habits of reading. Julio Cortázar, himself a champion reformer of reading habits, perceived the particular challenge of *Paradiso* when he wrote:

> What then can we expect from the "female reader" who confronts *Paradiso*, which as a character of Lewis Carroll's said, would try the patience of an oyster? But there is no patience where you start off with an absence of humility and hope, where a conditioned, prefabricated culture flattered by writers one could call functional, with rebellions and heterodoxies that are carefully delimited by the Marquesses of Queensberry of the profession, rejects any work that truly goes against the grain. Capable of facing any literary difficulty on the intellectual or the emotional plane so long as it keeps within the rules of the game of the West, ready to play the most arduous Proustian or Joycean games of chess which will entail familiar pieces and foreseeable strategies, this culture draws back in indignation and irony the moment it is invited to explore an extrageneric territory, to do battle with a language and a plot that correspond to a narrative system not born of books but out of long lessons of abyss.[2]

Cortázar is right. Lezama's purpose is to give his readers lessons at and about the abyss. His is a poetic brinksmanship that strikes no compromises with the reader, not even in the texts that purport to expound on his poetics. Lezama's essays, which have so much of the prose poem about them, recall those of Mallarmé, but they have nothing of the French poet's despair before the blank page.

Lezama's autodidacticism and erudition also present serious obstacles when one tries to situate him in the context of the history of literary theory. How does one establish an intellectual context for a writer who from a philosophical standpoint sometimes seems a contemporary of Dante, but who also at times offers insights that thirty years later have become commonplaces of literary thought? I believe that the most fruitful approach is to lay aside the claims that Lezama and some of his critics make regarding his poetic *system* and instead examine his actual *practice* of reading and writing, his practice of cultural consumption.

Perhaps the most disconcerting feature of Lezama's work is a practice of reading and writing that flies in the face of the Western literary tradition by dissolving the fundamental dichotomy between nature and culture. Mimetic and antimimetic poetics equally build their edifices on the distinction between art and nature despite their differences regarding the character of that relationship. Art either draws upon nature or proclaims its right to turn in upon itself. What shocks the reader of Lezama is not that his work draws equally upon nature and culture, but that he treats culture as other artists treat nature.

There are two fundamental reasons for this idiosyncratic attitude toward culture: one is related to Lezama's concept of poetic creation, and the other is rooted in his concept of Americanness. Poetic creation is, for him, totally centered on metaphorical expression, and both nature and culture serve as quarries for images. In his work the changing tides, the stars, a tumor, asthma, homosexuality, a madman endlessly circling a tree, all may be cast into emblems that will capture aspects of his poetic and ethical tenets, but so may the name of an artist, a novel, a painting, a historical figure, or a literary critic. Lezama's attitude toward culture can only be understood after grasping the very special meaning nature has for him. Nature is not the impassive, invincible antagonist of the naturalistic novels of the jungle like José Eustasio Rivera's *La vorágine* (*The Vortex*) or Mario Vargas Llosa's *La Casa Verde* (The Green House). It is also not the nature of Alejo Carpentier's "lo real maravilloso americano" ("the American marvelous real"), an attempt to view nature through the eyes of primitive people for whom the supernatural is still the viable explanation for natural phenomena.[3] González Echevarría explains that "Carpentier's concept of the marvelous or of magic rests on an onto-theological assumption: the existence of a peculiar Latin American consciousness devoid of self-reflexiveness and inclined to faith; a consciousness that allows Latin Americans to live immersed in culture and to feel history not as a causal process that can be analyzed rationally and intellectually, but as destiny" (*Alejo Carpentier*, p. 125).

González Echevarría also makes clear that Carpentier himself, by virtue of his self-reflexiveness, does not share that inclination to faith. Although it would be misleading to identify Lezama with the peculiar Latin American consciousness described by Carpentier, he does possess the faith his compatriot lacks. Lezama's view of nature also depends on theology, but his perspective is that of an adherent of the theological system, not the external viewpoint of the anthropologist. Nature for Lezama evokes Genesis, the garden of Eden, the fall of Adam and Eve. Poetry (or life; for Lezama it is one and the same) has as its goal the recuperation of that nature lost through original sin. His is a primarily Pascalian concept of nature, as he explains in the essay of *Tratados en la Habana* [*Treatises in Havana*], "Pascal y la poesía" ("Pascal and Poetry").

> *Hay inclusive como la obligación de devolver la naturaleza perdida. De fabricar naturaleza, no de recibirla como algo dado. "Como la verdadera naturaleza se ha perdido—dice Pascal—, todo puede ser naturaleza." La elaboración de la naturaleza en el hombre, que nada tiene que ver con el hombre como enfermedad o excepción de la naturaleza en los existencialistas. Si la pérdida de la naturaleza se debió al pecado, no lo puede ser en el hombre el afán de colocar en el sitio de la naturaleza después de la caída, otra naturaleza segregada o elaborada. En el sitio de esa naturaleza caída, enemiga del hombre, no se percibe un misterio ni una claridad, ni el misterio que desliza la sustancia de la fe ni la momentánea claridad que se deriva de penetrar en las esencias quiditarias (Obras completas, 2: 564)*

• • •

There is even the obligation to return the lost nature. To build nature, not to receive it as something given. "Since the true nature has been lost," says Pascal, "everything can be nature." The elaboration of nature within man, which has nothing to do with man as disease or exception of nature in the Existentialists. If the loss of nature was due to sin, the same is not true of man's yearning to put in the place of nature after the fall, another nature that has been elaborated or secreted. On the site of that fallen nature, the enemy of man, one can neither perceive a mystery nor a clarity, neither the mystery slipped in by the substance of faith nor the sudden clarity that comes from penetrating into quidditary essences.

Lezama takes the conventional Catholic notion of the fall and redemption of humankind and applies it to the practice of poetry. The nature we once had is lost; our task is to "elaborate," to "secrete" (one thinks of a pearl forming in an oyster) a new nature that will approximate the one we lost. Prior to that elaboration, nature is "fallen nature" and is incapable of either the mysteries of faith or the sudden revelations that are possible if we construct a new nature for ourselves. Nature must not be accepted as a given, it must undergo a transformation through art, which for Lezama means that it must be translated into cultural images, poetic images whose purpose is to give the poet and the reader access to the Image (referred to by Lezama as "la Imagen" or *"la imago"*), a concept that ties figurative language to mystic revelation. The following passage from "Mitos y cansancio clásico" ["Myths and Classical Weariness"] in *La expresión americana* [*American Expression*] deals with the transformation of natural entities into cultural ones:

> *Determinada masa de entidades naturales o culturales, adquieren en un súbito, inmensas resonancias. Entidades como las expresiones, fábulas milesias o ruinas de Pérgamo, adquieren en un espacio contrapunteado por la* imago *y el sujeto metafórico, nueva vida, como la planta o el espacio dominado. De ese espacio contrapunteado depende la metamorfosis de una entidad natural en cultural imaginaria. Si digo piedra, estamos en los dominios de una entidad natural, pero si digo piedra donde lloró Mario, en las ruinas de Cartago, constituimos una entidad cultural de sólida gravitación. La fuerza de urdimbre y la gravitación caracterizan ese espacio contrapunteado por la imago, que le presta la extensión* hasta donde ese espacio tiene fuerza animista en relación con esas entidades. *(2: 283)*

• • •

A given mass of natural or cultural entities unexpectedly acquires immense resonances. Entities like the expressions "Milesian fables" or "the ruins of Pergamum" acquire new life in a space in counterpoint with the *imago* and the metaphorical subject, like a plant or the space dominated. The metamorphosis of a natural entity into a cultural, imaginary one depends on that contrapuntal space. If I say "rock," we are in the realm of a natural entity, but if I say, "the rock on which Marius wept in the ruins of Carthage," we constitute a cultural entity of solid gravitation. Interconnective power and gravitation characterize the space that is in counterpoint with the *imago* which endows it with *extension* up to where that space has an animist force in relation to those entities.

Herein lies the complexity of Lezama's concept of nature and culture. Nature must not be accepted as a given, it must be created anew as culture, but that culture then is treated paradoxically by him as if it were a given. The concept of causality has no relevance to culture in his view. This has radical consequences for his practice of cultural consumption. Without causality there is no question of influence, and therefore no dynamic conception of culture. For Lezama the history of ideas has more to do with immanence than with evolution. Culture is composed of ideas and stances, autonomous emblems that echo and corroborate each other more in space than in time. This static concept of knowledge derives from Lezama's theological notion of truth, and its essential passivity responds to the mystic expectation of the bestowal of that truth in ecstasy if one achieves the required receptivity. For Lezama culture, therefore, is as much a given as nature is for most of us, and it is this attitude that explains both his view of literary influence and what appears to be his total lack of anxiety about that influence. The ego that humbles itself before God, hoping to effect a mystical union and attain the certainty of divine revelation, can have no anxiety of influence since the mystical union entails the total surrender of autonomy.

Lezama accords great importance to his practice of cultural consumption. In numerous essays and interviews, and in his novels, he has explored its consequences for humanity, Latin Americans, and Cubans in particular. Everywhere he has indicated its possible contributions to literature and to literary studies, a field that he feels has long gone astray. With antediluvian optimism, his essays decry and reject the pessimism of the poets and critics he considers "crepuscular": Mallarmé, Valéry, and Eliot in particular:

> *Sabemos que en el caso peculiar de T. S. Eliot, el método mítico era más bien mítico crítico, conforme a su neoclasicismo á outrance, que situaba en cada obra contemporánea la tarea de los glosadores para precisar su respaldo en épocas míticas, pues él es un crítico pesimista de la era crepuscular. Pesimista en cuanto él cree que la creación fue realizada por los antiguos y que a los contemporáneos solo nos resta el juego de las combinatorias. Es más, lo convierte en uno de los temas de su poema* East Coker *. . . Eliot pretende, en realidad, no acercarse a los nuevos mitos, con respecto a los cuales parece mostrarse dubitativo y reservado, o a la vivencia de los mitos ancestrales, sino el resguardo que ofrecen esos mitos a las obras contemporáneas, los que le otorgan como una nobleza clásica. Por eso, su crítica es esencialmente pesimista o crepuscular, pues él cree que los maestros antiguos no pueden ser sobrepasados, quedando tan solo la fruición de repetir, tal vez con nuevo acento. Apreciación cercana al pesimismo spengleriano y al*

eterno retorno que asegura en la finitud de las combinatorias, el posible
ricorsi. *(2: 285–286)*

. . .

We know that in the particular case of T. S. Eliot the mythical method
was more than anything mythico-critical in accordance with his Neo-
classicism *à outrance* which saw in each contemporary work a labor of
glossers seeking for support in mythical eras, since he is a pessimistic
critic of the crepuscular era. He is a pessimist in so far as he believes
that creation was carried out by the ancients and that we contemporaries have nothing left but games of combinations. Moreover, he makes
this one of the themes of his poem "East Coker" . . . What Eliot really
wants to do is not to approach new myths, toward which he seems to feel
doubtful and reserved, or the experience of ancestral myths, but rather
the shelter that those myths offer contemporary works upon which they
bestow a kind of classical nobility. His criticism is essentially pessimistic or crepuscular because he believes that the ancient masters cannot be surpassed and that all that remains is the pleasure of repeating,
perhaps with a new accent. A viewpoint close to Spenglerian pessimism
and the eternal return that it assures through the finitude of combinations, the possible *ricorsi*.

Unlike his contemporary Jorge Luis Borges, whose position could
be admirably encompassed by Lezama's phrase "all that remains is
the pleasure of repeating, perhaps with a new accent" (that "perhaps" is Borges's trademark), Lezama categorically rejects the concept of a "literature of exhaustion."[4] Lezama's response to European
exhaustion and pessimism is his optimism regarding the unlimited
creative powers of humanity:

> *Nuestro método quisiera más acercarse a esa técnica de la ficción, pre-*
> *conizada por Curtius, que al método mítico crítico de Eliot. Todo*
> *tendrá que ser reconstruido, invencionado de nuevo, y los viejos mitos,*
> *al reaparecer de nuevo, nos ofrecerán sus conjuros y sus enigmas con*
> *un rostro desconocido. La ficción de los mitos son nuevos mitos, con*
> *nuevos cansancios y terrores. (2: 286)*[5]

. . .

Our method would rather approach that technique of fiction proposed
by Curtius than Eliot's method of myth criticism. Everything will have
to be rebuilt, reinvented, and the old myths as they reappear again will
offer us their spells and their enigmas with an unknown face. The fiction of myths constitutes new myths with new wearinesses and terrors.

To understand further an optimism that seems scandalous even by mid-twentieth-century standards, it is helpful to examine Lezama's devaluation of the concept of literary influence. In an important interview with Ciro Bianchi Ross, Lezama suggests that the question of literary influence has been oversimplified and perceived in a misleadingly mechanistic fashion:

> *El problema de las influencias es casi inapresable porque el hombre es un instante sensorial infinitamente polarizado. A veces una palabra, una sentencia apenas entreoída nos ilumina y logra configurar formas de expresión. Casi siempre lo que apenas conocemos es lo que logra influenciarnos, después volvemos, insistimos, adquirimos tal vez lo que los pedantes llaman conocimiento exhaustivo, pero ya eso no produce en nosotros resonancias ni vibraciones.[6]*
>
> • • •
>
> The problem of influences is almost ungraspable because man is an infinitely polarized sensorial instant. Sometimes a word, a barely heard phrase illuminates us and manages to fashion forms of expression. Almost always what we barely know is what actually influences us, later we return, we insist, we acquire what pedants call exhaustive knowledge, but that no longer produces resonances or vibrations in us.

A critique of the notion of literary influence would certainly find adherents in the contemporary theoretical arena, but few would subscribe to the alternative Lezama proposes. Here Lezama articulates the bedrock belief in the epiphanic character of artistic creation that is central to his understanding and practice of literature as both reader and writer. In literature as well as in life, he believes that truth is not attained by exhaustive research and the discipline of logic. These in fact obscure the path to the truth and can make one lose valuable, initial insights. This contention recalls the remark of another poet who was very concerned with the object and the methods of literary criticism, T. S. Eliot. In "Tradition and the Individual Talent" he observes, "It will even be affirmed that much learning deadens or perverts poetic sensibility."[7] At least in this instance, Eliot and Lezama seem to agree. For Lezama the path to truth is rather a discipline of receptiveness: truth is dispensed in the manner of spiritual grace to those who open themselves to it. Although Lezama enriches it with Oriental resonances, in particular those of Zen Buddhism, his antirational concept of illumination is essentially Christian and has its roots in the thought of St. Augustine. Truth cannot be wrested by the mind but instead must be received—

according to the Augustinian metaphor—by listening with "the ear of the heart."[8]

Lezama's contention that exhaustive knowledge based on careful reading is less likely to prove influential or illuminating than what we barely know radically challenges the concept of literary influence and the most basic precepts of literary historicism. By privileging intuition over erudition, this view of the relation between authors and literature effectively erases the distinction between readings and misreadings. In his understanding of influence Lezama seems closest to Harold Bloom, who in *The Anxiety of Influence* asserts: "Poetic Influence—when it involves two strong, authentic poets,—always proceeds by a misreading of the prior poet, an act of creative correction that is actually and necessarily a misinterpretation."[9] Lezama's preference for the isolated "half-heard" phrase effectively denies a role to context in literary interpretation. For him the text's only valid context is the consciousness of the reader. Consequently, the only valid literary tradition is the heterogeneous assembly of texts with which the reader maintains a running intellectual dialogue throughout life. The threads that bind these texts into what must be described oxymoronically as "a personal literary tradition" are the lasting preoccupations of each reader, and the place where the dialogue takes place is in the reader's memory. As Santí explains: "But, although it is true that Lezama wants to rescue the intrinsic approach, he does not intend to reduce reading to those terms. He then introduces the need for a reading of the tradition in the text by means of the mediating function of memory" ("Lezama, Vitier y la crítica de la razón reminiscente," p. 537).

The inversion of the cause-and-effect relationship is Lezama's favorite iconoclastic response to the strictures of traditional influence study. He argues that great artists reinvent their sources and their influences, and that, therefore, it is illusory to speak of the influence of Maurice Scève on Mallarmé, or of the Marquis de Saint-Simon and the *Arabian Nights* on Proust:

> *Las influencias no son de causas que engendran efectos, sino de efectos que iluminan causas. Proust hace que se lean las* Memorias de Saint-Simon *o que se vuelva al sentido del relato de* Las mil y una noches, *como una consecuencia de un acto excepcional, pero desgraciadamente los profesores, que son los gendarmes obligados de estos temas, gustan más de las cadenas causales que de las iluminaciones. La impregnación, la conjugación, la genminaridad son formas de creación más sutiles que los desarrollos causales.*[10]

• • •

Influences are not causes that engender effects, but effects that illuminate causes. Proust makes us read the *Memoirs* of Saint-Simon or makes
us return to the *Arabian Nights'* concept of the narrative as a consequence of an exceptional act. But unfortunately, professors who are the
inevitable *gendarmes* of these topics prefer causal chains to illuminations. Impregnation, conjugation, geminarity are more subtle forms of
creation than causal developments.

Once more, Lezama downgrades causality according priority to the
creative spark and to the processes that foster its appearance: "impregnation," "conjugation," and "geminarity" (a word apparently
coined by Lezama that seems to combine the concepts of germi-
nation and twinness or homology). These three processes are part
of the central poetic activities he calls "creative assimilation" and
"retrospective imagination."

Beyond its strictly creative function, "creative assimilation" is
endowed by Lezama with an ethnic dimension; it is the essential
cultural trait that defines Americanness. He maintains that it is a
particular characteristic of American writers, an outgrowth of the
historical experience of colonialism. As participants in European
culture only through the illegitimate inheritance of colonization,
American writers are, in Lezama's view, free to partake of any cultural tradition that attracts them without committing themselves.
In order to clarify this American prerogative, he contrasts the attitudes of two European writers to Goethe with his own stance:

> *Pero todo se reduce al* simpathos, *habrá siempre los que amen a Goethe*
> *(al llegar a cierto grado la admiración es una forma del amor, del Eros*
> *cognoscente) y los que lo detesten. En nuestra época, por ejemplo, Gide*
> *lo ama, Claudel lo detesta. Pero yo como americano, puedo permitirme*
> *otra voluptuosidad inteligente, admirar a Claudel, y amar a Goethe.*
> *De la misma manera que Martí pudo admirar y amar a Whitman y a*
> *Goethe. Gide y Claudel admiraban a Whitman, pero bifurcaban trá-*
> *gicamente en Goethe. Martí como americano, podía permitirse ese es-*
> *plendor de la asimilación creadora.*[11]
>   • • •

But it all comes down to *sympathos,* there will always be people who
love Goethe (when it reaches a certain point admiration is a form of
love, of a knowing Eros) and those who detest him. In our day, for example, Gide loves him, Claudel hates him. But I, as an American, can
allow myself another intelligent voluptuousness, to admire Claudel and
love Goethe. In the same manner that Martí could admire and love
Whitman and Goethe. Gide and Claudel admired Whitman, but they

tragically parted company on Goethe. Martí as an American could allow himself that splendor of creative assimilation.

The paradigm of José Martí as a quintessential American writer recurs in Lezama's writings, not as one would expect because of Martí's ideology, but because Lezama considers him a kindred spirit and a master of "creative assimilation."

Julio Cortázar admired and seemingly envied Lezama's ability to assimilate disparate literary traditions without committing himself to any particular one. His essay "Para llegar a Lezama Lima" ("To Reach Lezama Lima") dwells with almost obsessive intensity on the profound Americanness of Lezama's worldview. In Lezama Cortázar discovers (or thinks he discovers) a primitive artist living in a state of creative grace.[12] From the point of view of a European writer (with whom Cortázar identifies) who considers himself a latecomer to a cultural tradition that has exhausted all creative avenues, Lezama is in an enviable position:

> Between the knowledge of Lezama and that of a European (or his River Plate homologues, much less American in the respect to which I allude) there is the difference that separates innocence from guilt. Every European writer is "slave to his baptism," if I may paraphrase Rimbaud. Whether he wants it or not, his decision to write entails shouldering an immense and almost fearsome tradition. Whether he accepts it or fights against it, that tradition inhabits him; it is his familiar, his incubus. Why should he write if in a sense all has been written? . . . Meanwhile on his island Lezama awakens with pre-Adamic joy . . . and he does not feel guilty of any direct tradition. He assumes them all, from the livers of the Etruscans to Leopold Bloom blowing his nose on a dirty hand-kerchief, but without historical commitment, without being a French or an Austrian writer. He is a Cuban with a mere fistful of his own culture on his back and the rest is knowledge pure and free, not career responsibility. He can write whatever he feels like writing without having to tell himself that Rabelais already, that Martial . . . He is not a link in the chain, he is not obligated to do more, better, or different; he does not have to justify himself as a writer. ("Para llegar a Lezama Lima," pp. 54–56)

The Argentinian rejoices that the literary tradition does not hang like an albatross from the Cuban's neck. Free from the European chains of causality, Lezama rearranges literary constellations with impunity, creating new patterns in the mosaic of the literary tradition.

As reader, writer, and literary essayist Lezama employs the same basic technique: juxtaposition (perhaps what he would call "conjugation," activating the etymological sense of the word: a yoking together). Through the juxtaposition of unexpected elements (imagery in his poetry, literary works in his essays and novels) he hopes to provoke the spark of revelation. These contrapuntal groupings which at first may jar the reader as capricious very often yield insights in his hands. Anticipating resistance, Lezama defends his method from the charge of arbitrariness in the essay "A partir de la poesía" ("Starting from Poetry"):

> *Fulgurantes agrupamientos, que en un instante o en cualquier unidad de tiempo, establecen como una clave, una familia, una semejanza en lo errante o inadvertido. Claves que no existen en una demorada casa temporal, sino impuestas por una circunstancia, un agrupamiento aparentemente caprichoso o fatal, pero que establece una división por gestos o actitudes, por acudimientos o inhibiciones, tan importantes, dentro de ese breve reducto temporal, como una reorganización por lo económico, por las exigencias del trabajo, o por los linajes que se fundan o se suceden. Nada más lejos de poder contentarnos con la creencia de que son agrupamientos banales o dictados por el capricho.* (2: 827)

. . .

Flashing groupings which in an instant or in any unit of time establish a kind of key, a family, a similarity within what is errant or unnoticed. Keys that do not exist in a tardy temporal house but are imposed by a circumstance, an apparently capricious or fatal grouping. But one that establishes a division through gestures or attitudes, through outreaches or inhibitions, as important within this brief temporal redoubt as a reorganization because of economics, because of the demands of work, or because of the lineages that are founded or continued. Nothing could be further from us than the mere satisfaction of believing that these are just banal groupings or that they are dictated simply by whim.

The flashing groupings, according to Lezama, offer a key by virtue of the homologies that are foregrounded by the imposed circumstance (the grouping by the poet). Lezama's ultimate defense of his method, therefore, derives from its practice and its results.

The figure of José Martí, the father of the Cuban nation, the dominant figure of Cuban letters, the man who forged the concept of Cubanness against which Cubans have since measured themselves, naturally looms large in the thought of Lezama. It is difficult to assess the degree to which the literary and ethical model of "The

them, but they were not in my memory. Then where were they? Or how
was it that, when I heard them spoken, I recognized them and said:
"That is right. That is true," unless in fact they were in my memory
already, but so far back and so buried, as it were, in the furthest recesses
that, if they had not been dragged out by the suggestion of someone else,
I should perhaps not have been able to conceive of them? (p. 221)

Santí has explained the vital role that memory plays in the epistemology of the *Orígenes* group. Developed in the essays Lezama
and Cintio Vitier published in *Orígenes* and other journals, the
focus on the function of memory in poetry gives their theoretical
writings a direction: "A critical direction that springs from the
meditation about poetry as the source and method of knowledge at
whose center a series of important though little studied texts situ-
ates the mediating function of memory, of reconstructive, creative
reminiscence within time" ("Lezama, Vitier, y la crítica," p. 535). It
is not difficult to see the close relationship between the concept of
"creative assimilation" that we have been discussing and "reconstructive reminiscence," the role of memory in that process of assimilation. Lezama's process of "reconstructive reminiscence" must
be understood in terms of the Christian tradition of figural interpretation explained by Erich Auerbach:[13] "Figural interpretation establishes a connection between two events or persons, the first of
which signifies not only itself but also the second, while the second
encompasses or fulfills the first. The two poles of the figure are separate in time, but both, being real events or figures, are within time,
within the stream of historical life" ("Figura," p. 53). In accordance
with the structure of figural interpretation, Lezama's vision of Pérez
and Martí is at the same time historical and allegorical: "Since in
figural interpretation one thing stands for another, since one thing
represents and signifies the other, figural interpretation is "allegorical" in the widest sense. But it differs from most of the allegorical forms known to us by the historicity both of the sign and what it
signifies" (p. 54).

The seemingly arbitrary juxtaposition of the literary styles of two
men separated by three centuries is in fact a complex and rich poetic
maneuver through which Lezama "conjugates" (to use his term) not
only the styles of Martí and Pérez but also the emblematic historical
value of both men.[14] During his exile in Spain, Martí lived in Saragossa and witnessed its gallant and useless defense of the Republic
in 1874. This biographical fact reminds Lezama of the revolt in defense of the *fueros* (privileges) of Aragon motivated by Pérez's flight

Apostle" (as Martí is known in Cuba) shaped Lezama's own
itinerary and influenced his role as the artistic leader of his
tion. Nevertheless, it is clear that Lezama is attracted by
traits of Martí's prose style, and a poetic use of history and
constructs that is very similar to his own.

It, therefore, seems appropriate to choose an essay about l
order to illustrate Lezama's contrapuntal or juxtapositional
of reading. The fact that the essay in question sets out to sub
concept of literary influence further confirms the choice. L
essay "Influencias en busca de Martí" ("Influences in S(
Martí") offers an excellent model of "creative assimilation'
the same time, clarifies the meaning of Lezama's phrase "eff(
illuminate causes." Its very title already reveals the gesture
Lezama seeks to elude the chain of cause and effect. In this
1955, he searches for resonances of Martí's prose style in th
of Antonio Pérez, the powerful secretary of Philip II of Spain
pating by eighteen years the concept of *apophrades* (i.e., tl
poets sometimes manage to give the impression that thei
sors imitate their style) articulated by Harold Bloom in *The*
of Influence, Lezama senses the "mark" of Martí in the l
Antonio Pérez.

A close study of the essay reveals the complex opera
Lezama's "retrospective imagination." Although the comp
Martí and Pérez actually depends on the very issue of influel
least the supposition that the Cuban poet must have read
Pérez during his stay in Saragossa, Lezama deemphasizes th
in favor of "geminarity" (twinness). Thus, Martí's reading o
not taken to be the first step in a process of imitation but
moment of revelation. Upon reading the Renaissance cou
Cuban poet does not choose him as a model, but rather reco
"remembers" his own style in Pérez's prose.

This concept of knowledge as remembrance once mor
Lezama's affinity for the thought of St. Augustine, whose
knowledge and illumination depends on the particular c(
memory described in Book 10 of the *Confessions:*

> From where, then, and how did they [sensory images] enter int
> memory? I do not know. For when I learned them, I was not ta
> them on trust from some other mind; I was recognizing them i
> own mind; I accepted them as true and committed them to m;
> though I were depositing them in some place where I could fin
> again whenever I wanted. So they were in my mind, even before

from prison in Madrid to Saragossa.[15] Lezama exploits this circumstance in the essay:

Entonces llegó a lo que Antonio Pérez había dejado con caballos voladores y el peso de sus secretos, para apoderarse de la herencia del motín popular, José Martí. No recoge la lengua escrita de Baltasar Gracián, sino las órdenes y avisos que Antonio Pérez transparentaba a través de los tabiques carcelarios para avivar la espera de los amotinados de afuera. La lengua de Antonio Pérez es la de las cartas y la de los consejos que da a reyes y a principales. El idioma conversa, con las interrupciones que le sueltan los escuchas en personas o en sombra, traza nudillos por el aliento varonil y sentencias extraídas con la yesca de la averiguación inmediata y presente.

  En Zaragoza, Martí siente las vivencias del destierro de Antonio Pérez. La obsequiosidad principal y la tierna despedida en las cartas del secretario, deben haber sido leídas por Martí, avivadas las junturas de ambos destierros. "Señora, si hubiese por allá unas manos—le dice a la hermana del Bearnés, que es de quien más se fía—,guárdemelas V. A.; que las he menester más que un manco." Cómo Martí sentiría esos bandazos suaves, esos toques resbalantes y cariciosos, donde su ternura parece adquirir la textura de una piel clásica y de buena compañía. En otra carta enviada a Enrique IV, rompe su escritura con esos creados halagos cariñosos, tan del gusto de Martí: "Envío a V. M. el agua de los ojos del alma, Señor, y de las entrañas mías la destilaría yo muy alegre para vuestra salud y vida; sino que estoy ya todo seco, y aun para una destilación, inútil ya. De donde me vengo a aborrecer yo mismo, porque cuando no soy de provecho para quien amo, no me querría ver." (2: 504–505)

• • •

Then José Martí came to what Antonio Pérez had left with flying horses and the weight of his secrets, to seize the inheritance of the popular uprising. He does not pick up the written language of Baltasar Gracián, but the orders and warnings that Antonio Pérez spirited through the prison walls in order to enliven the wait of the insurgents outside. The language of Antonio Pérez is that of the letters and the counsel that he gives to kings and heads of state. The language converses, with the interruptions flung to it by the sentries, through persons or in the shadow; it traces knots through the manly breath and sentences that have been extracted with the flint of immediate and present inquiry.

  In Saragossa, Martí shares the personal experiences of Antonio Pérez's exile. The principal courteousness and the tender farewell in the letters of the Secretary must have been read by Martí, brought to life by the conjunction of both exiles. "My lady, should there happen to be some hands there," he says to the sister of the Duke of Bearn, who is among those he trusts most, "keep them for me, Your Highness, for I have more need of them than a maimed man." How Martí must have felt those soft heavings, those sliding and caressing touches where his tenderness seems to acquire the texture of a classical skin and of good company. In another letter sent to Henri IV, his writing sets off with those created, affectionate pieces of flattery that were so much to Martí's taste: "I send Your Majesty the water from the eyes of my soul, My Lord, and even from my entrails would I happily distill it for the sake of your health and life, but that I am already all dry, and even useless for a distillation. Therefore do I come to abhor myself, because when I am of no profit to those I love, I cannot bear my own sight."

The association of Martí and Pérez in political terms, unthinkable from the viewpoint of contemporary historians, is perfectly plausible given the interpretation romantic historians gave the deeds of 1591. Gregorio Marañón has commented on the romantic deformation of the actual significance of the *fueros:*

> The prestige of the *Fueros* and of the so-called liberties of Aragon, out of which the nineteenth century created a true intangible myth, was not totally deserved. It was forgotten that although those *Fueros*, generally speaking, sheltered the country from the possible excesses of the supreme power—from the kings of Aragon itself before its union with Castille, and from the Court of Madrid after that union—they were decrees that favored, more than the people themselves, the almost all-embracing power of the local lords over their vassals. The excellent liberal historians with the inevitable prejudices of their time were incapable of seeing this, or in the case of those who did see, of confessing it. Even today there are many who balk when it is affirmed that the *Fueros* of Aragon were the instruments used against tradesmen and field laborers by a minority that proved unworthy of them, and that by attacking those *Fueros*, the absolute monarchs were not perceived as tyrants by those below because the people felt much more the tyranny of the local lords, and for them it was a relief to join the central power.[16]

These liberal historians whom Marañón chastises are, of course, the historians who shaped Martí's concept of Spanish history. They, like Martí, projected their antimonarchism and their struggle for a republic (in Spain and in Cuba respectively) onto what had been, in essence, a struggle between recalcitrant feudal lords and a monarch who was trying to solidify an emerging national state. For Martí and the liberal historians, however, there was no room for doubt: the Aragonese and in particular the Saragossans were protorepublicans fighting against the tyranny of Philip II, and Antonio Pérez's role as instigator of the short-lived and ill-fated revolt was seen as a valiant act of patriotism rather than a fallen statesman's desperate attempt to save his life.

For Martí, Philip II, more than a historical figure, was a cultural emblem that embodied all that was wrong with Spain not only in the sixteenth century but throughout time. An article published by *La Opinión Nacional* (*The National Opinion*) of Caracas on December 28, 1881, where Martí reports on current events in Spain, furnishes an excellent example of his application of emblems taken from Habsburg Spain to contemporary events. The article, which in several features recalls the essays of Lezama, shows Martí to be an adept master of "creative assimilation."

La revolución que ha tomado del brazo al Monarca, procura arrebatarlo a sus huestes naturales y apartarlo de su vieja silla de oro, y la Iglesia, madre de la Monarquía, fulmina sus anatemas contra la revolución. Los nobles andan divididos y se amparan los unos de la Iglesia y los otros movidos de aquel espíritu que animó a Juan de Lanuza y halló feliz forma poética en García del Castañar, combaten en el campo nuevo. . . . Que el Rey viva para su nación y la gran masa humilde, quiere el precepto liberal, y el precepto conservador quiere que la nación viva para el Rey, y para el mantenimiento de su séquito. . . . La libertad, que tiene fe en sí, aguarda. Las instituciones viejas, que van perdiendo la fe, se exaltan y provocan. . . . Intentan sofocar la voz de la naturaleza humana. Blanden aún el estandarte verde de los autos de fe. Besarían aún, con labios amantes la mano huesosa y fría de aquel monarca tenebroso y lívido. . . . Las instituciones viejas acaparan las armaduras oxidadas de los Museos Reales, las carrozas carcomidas de Juana la Loca y Carlos II, las estatuas de piedra de los monarcas góticos, los atriles gigantescos que sustentan en bordado espaldar de bronce misales corpulentos, en cuyas páginas de rugoso pergamino dibujaron letras negras y rojas los monjes demacrados y sombríos de Zurbarán y Ribera; y con todas esas históricas riquezas alzan barricada a la cohorte batalladora de la época, que viene calle arriba, en gran tren de vapor, cargada de piquetes, de arados, de libros, de buques, de dragas, de limas que rebajan montes, de botones eléctricos que hacen volar islas, de cuchillas que sajan las cordilleras y echan a hervir juntos en la colosal herida los apartados y rugientes mares![17]

• • •

The revolution, which has taken the Monarch by the arm, seeks to tear
him from his natural followers and to draw him away from his old gilt
chair, and the Church, mother of the Monarchy, hurls fulminating anath-
emas at the revolution. The nobles are divided and some seek the protection of the Church while others, moved by that spirit which drove
Juan de Lanuza and found a felicitous poetic form in García del Castañar,
fight in the new field. . . . The liberal precept wants the King to live for
his country and for the great humble masses, and the conservative precept wants the country to live for the King and for the maintenance of
his retinue. . . . Liberty, which has faith in itself, waits. The old institutions, which are losing the faith, grow agitated and provocative. . . .
They try to smother the voice of human nature. They still brandish the
green banner of the autos da fe. They would still kiss with loving lips
the bony and cold hand of that gloomy and livid monarch. . . . The old
institutions hoard the rusty suits of armor of the Royal Museums, the
worm-eaten carriages of Joan the Mad and Charles II, the stone statues
of the Gothic monarchs, the gigantic lecterns which sustain on their
bronze tracery backs corpulent missals on whose pages of wrinkled
parchment the emaciated and somber monks of Zurbarán and Ribera
drew black and red letters; and with all these historical riches they raise
a barricade against the battling cohort of our times which is coming up
the street in a great steam train, loaded with pickets, plows, books,
ships, dredges, files that shave down mountains, electric buttons that
blow up islands, blades that cut mountain ranges and set the separate
and roaring seas to boil in the colossal wound!

Arguing for the inevitability of the move toward constitutional
monarchy, Martí depicts the contenders by means of two sets of images (an example of "restrospective imagination" worthy of Lezama):
conservative Spain is represented by Philip II, the Inquisition, and
the Church, which is morbidly evoked by the composite image of
Zurbarán's and Ribera's monks and the beautiful but threatening
lecterns. Conservative Spain is opposed by the avalanche of the
modern, populist, technological world. The threatening missals are
countered by modern books and the worm-eaten royal carriages by
the futuristic images of trains, steamships, canal-digging steam-
shovels, and electric buttons that destroy whole islands! Here Martí's
enthusiasm for modern technology recalls Jules Verne, who, as Cortázar has demonstrated, is a favorite author of Lezama's.[18]
But Lezama's style is everywhere in this passage: in Martí's enthusiastic avalanche of elaborate images and particularly in the evo-
cation not so much of the Spanish monks of history as those of

Zurbarán's and Ribera's paintings, in the sensuality that cannot resist the temptation to pause and observe the intricacy of a bronze lectern, the texture of parchment, and the complexion of painted monks—and that hyperbolic electric button that blows up islands is a "retrospective echo" of Lezama's well-known image of the electric switch that unexpectedly turns on Niagara Falls instead of the light in a room. All these features bear the "mark" of Lezama, or at least betray influences in search of Lezama.

Martí's poem "Para Aragón en España" ("For Aragon in Spain") is never mentioned in Lezama's "Influences in Search of Martí" but it is unquestionably the text that motivates the link between Pérez and Martí. It is the subtext, the matrix, upon which Lezama constructs his juxtapositional reading. In Martí's poetic and ideological vision of history there were two Spains at war with each other since the sixteenth century: the tyrannical, backward-looking Spain of Philip II and the populist, freedom-loving Spain that he saw embodied particularly by the rebellious history of Saragossa and the independent character of the Aragonese (such as Juan de Lanuza, a protagonist of the 1591 revolt). The first Spain he fought zealously with words and actions from his arrest as an adolescent until his death in battle. For the second Spain he felt a deep kinship, and he vigorously defended it against the chauvinism of his compatriots. Although this dual concept of Spain is a constant in his works, nowhere is his defense of the freedom-loving Spain as deeply felt as in the well-known *Verso sencillo* VII (*Simple Verse* VII):

> *Para Aragón, en España,*
> *Tengo yo en mi corazón*
> *Un lugar todo Aragón,*
> *Franco, fiero, fiel, sin saña.*
>
> *Si quiere un tonto saber*
> *Por qué lo tengo, le digo*
> *Que allí tuve un buen amigo,*
> *Que allí quise a una mujer.*
>
> *Allá, en la vega florida,*
> *La de la heroica defensa,*
> *Por mantener lo que piensa*
> *Juega la gente la vida.*
>
> *Y si un alcalde lo aprieta*
> *O lo enoja un rey cazurro,*

Calza su manta el baturro
Y muere con su escopeta.

Quiero a la tierra amarilla
Que baña el Ebro lodoso:
Quiero el Pilar azuloso
De Lanuza y de Padilla.

Estimo a quien de un revés
Echa por tierra a un tirano:
Lo estimo, si es un cubano;
Lo estimo, si aragonés.

Amo los patios sombríos
Con escaleras bordadas;
Amo las naves calladas
Y los conventos vacíos.

Amo la tierra florida,
Musulmana o española,
Donde rompió su corola
La poca flor de mi vida.

．．．

For Aragon, in Spain,
I have in my heart
A place wholly Aragon,
Frank, fierce, faithful, rageless.

If a fool wants to know
Why I have it, I answer
That there I had a good friend,
That there I loved a woman.

There, in the flowering meadow,
Of the heroic defense,
To uphold their beliefs,
People stake their lives.

And if a mayor harasses
Or a sullen king angers him,
The Aragon peasant dons his cloak
And dies with his shotgun.

I love the yellow land
Bathed by the muddy Ebro:
I love the blue Pilar
Of Lanuza and Padilla.

I esteem whoever turns and
Brings down a tyrant:

> I esteem him, if he is Cuban;
> I esteem him, if Aragonese.
>
> I love the somber patios
> With tracery stairways;
> I love the silent naves
> And the empty convents.
>
> I love the flowering land,
> Moslem or Spanish,
> Where my life's scarce flower
> Burst its bloom.

The poem captures both Martí's ideological adhesion to the historical traditions of Aragon and his strong emotive bonds for a city where he was happy. He alludes to the events of 1591, as in the article in *La Opinión Nacional*, through Juan de Lanuza, the youthful *justicia* of Aragon executed by Philip II in the bloody suppression of the revolt.

The poem also offers another example of the *"genminaridad"* between Martí and Lezama. No commentator of Martí has been able to associate the Padilla mentioned in the poem with Aragon. The only relevant historical figure would seem to be Juan de Padilla, one of the leaders of the Comuneros revolt, but he was from Toledo (Castile) and was executed by Charles V in 1521.[19] If, as it appears, Martí made a mistake, it is a very interesting one, since he is historically wrong but thematically (emblematically) correct. The revolt of the Comuneros during the reign of Charles V is roughly analogous to the revolt over the *fueros* in Aragon during his son's reign. Both Lanuza and Padilla are therefore emblems of regional defiance against the crown and victims of autocracy. Martí's mistake is also interesting for another reason: it is precisely the type of mistake Lezama is wont to make. Lezama may err in the facts but seldom in the symbolic exploitation of those facts.

Finally, through the allusion to the heroic defense, Martí evokes another glorious moment in the history of Saragossa, the city's desperate defense against Napoleon's invading army. In a manner that recalls Lezama's associative cluster (Saragossa, rebellion, exile, antiroyalist struggle, letters of exiles) in "Influences in Search of Martí," in this "Simple Verse" Martí has gathered all the components necessary to establish the ideologically desirable equation between Aragonese and Cubans: "I esteem whoever turns and / Brings down a tyrant: / I esteem him if he is Cuban; / I esteem him, if Aragonese." Lezama's emblematic and poetic use of historical figures is prefigured by Martí's own emblematic use of history.

"Influences in Search of Martí" contains a phrase that could have been written by Bakhtin so much does it seem to capture his dialogical concept of language: "Language converses" ["El idioma conversa"] (p. 504). Santí has noted the undeniable affinity between Lezama's mode of reading as formulated in the 1941 essay "Julián del Casal" (2: 65–99) and the "dialogical principle" of the Russian formalist: " . . . the contrapuntal reading of language that Lezama describes goes beyond the study of sources at this point in order to inquire into the dialogical layers of poetic language—'the mystery of the echo'—which involves ascertaining the function of the intertextual connection. One might add that in this sense there is a curious affinity between the method here sketched out by Lezama and the dialogical classification put into practice twelve years before him by the formalist Mikhail Bakhtin" ("Lezama, Vitier, y la crítica," p. 538).

Neither is the "dialogical principle" the only similarity shared by the Cuban poet and the Russian thinker. Bakhtin's body of writings also resembles Lezama's essays because of its absence of systematization (the greatest problem for students of Bakhtin) and its persistence of themes. About this aspect of Bakhtin's works Tzvetan Todorov has written:

> . . . properly speaking, there is no *development* in Bakhtin's work. Bakhtin does change his focus; sometimes he alters his formulations, but, from his first to his last text, from 1922 to 1974, his thinking remains fundamentally the same; one can even find identical sentences written fifty years apart. Instead of development, there is *repetition,* a repetition obviously sectional for the most part, a sifting over and over of the same themes. Bakhtin's writings are more akin to elements of a series than to the components of a progressively erected construction; each one contains, in a way, the whole of his thought.[20]

Finally, both Lezama and Bakhtin exude an optimism that is rooted in their religious faith and in their mystical perspective on language and literature. There is, of course, no question of Bakhtin's influence on Lezama, since his works would have been linguistically and physically inaccessible to Lezama in 1941 and 1955 when he wrote the essays in question. Instead, the parallel between the thought of the Cuban writer and the Russian formalist remarkably attests to the validity of their insights. In human language and in thought there is a dialogue which does not depend on a simple matter of influence.

While doing research on Antonio Pérez, I myself experienced an

Augustinian moment of recognition such as Lezama must have felt upon reading the secretary's letters and sensing the *"genminaridad"* between his style and Martí's. In Marañón's book, I read: "Pérez learned, says the Conde de Luna, 'that since they had arrived to torture him, *the flower of his life had lost its bloom* ["era descoronada la flor de su vida"] and that his punishment would be carried out very soon; and he resolved to escape from the jail'" (*Antonio Pérez,* 1: 471; emphasis added). I remembered that the Conde de Luna's metaphor was also a metaphor of Martí's, the one he employs to characterize what in his case was a happy stay in Aragon: "Where my life's scarce flower / Burst its bloom." ["Donde rompió su corola / La poca flor de mi vida."] Lezama would doubtless have laughed and exclaimed, "The language converses."

Like Bakhtin, Lezama feels that the "conversation of the language" in literature should be the primary goal of literary criticism, and he has José Cemí, the protagonist of *Paradiso,* proclaim it in a key passage of Chapter 9:

La crítica ha sido muy burda en nuestro idioma. Al espíritu especioso de Menéndez y Pelayo, brocha gorda que desconoció siempre el barroco, que es lo que interesa de España y de España en América, es para él un tema ordalía, una prueba de arsénico y de frecuente descaro. De ahí hemos pasado a la influencia del seminario alemán de filología. Cogen desprevenido a uno de nuestros clásicos y estudian en él las cláusulas trimembres acentuadas en la segunda sílaba. Pero penetrar a un escritor en el centro de su contrapunto, como hace un Thibaudet con Mallarmé, en su estudio donde se va con gran precisión de la palabra al ámbito de la Orplid, eso lo desconocen beatíficamente. Por ejemplo, en Góngora, es frecuente la alusión a las joyas incaicas, sin embargo, no se ha estudiado la relación de Góngora con el inca Garcilaso, en el tiempo en que ambos coincidieron en Córdoba. Los incas en la imaginación de Góngora; he ahí un delicioso tema. . . . La imaginación retrospectiva, tan fundamental como cuando crea mundo o simples planetas zumbantes, tiene un placer interminable, los relatos que le hacía el inca Garcilaso a Góngora de una de las eras imaginarias, la tierra despidiendo imágenes, tienen que haber sobresaltado los sentidos del racionero mayor, en el momento en que se llevaba una enorme ración para su metáfora y su venablera. (1: 336–337)

• • •

Criticism in our literature has been very crude. The specious spirit of Menéndez y Pelayo, a thick brush that never understood the baroque, which is what has real interest in Spain and in Hispanic America, considered it an ordeal theme, a trial by arsenic and frequent impudence.

From that point we've [passed on to] the influence of German philological seminars, where they [take] one of our classics [by surprise] and go
through it for clauses having three elements with the accent on the second syllable. But penetrating a writer in the center of his counterpoint,
the way Thibaudet does with Mallarmé in the study where he goes with
great precision from words to the realm of Mörike's Orplid, is a matter
of beatific ignorance with them. For example, in Góngora there are frequent allusions to Inca jewels, but they still haven't studied the relations between Góngora and the Inca Garcilaso during the time they
were both in Córdova. 'Incas in the imagination of Góngora.' That's a
[delicious] topic. . . . [Retrospective] imagination, so fundamental when
it creates a world or simple buzzing planets, is endlessly pleasing, the
tales told by the Inca Garcilaso to Góngora about one of the imaginary
[eras], the earth emitting images, must have aroused the senses of the
great prebendary at the moment he was gathering together vast prebends
for his metaphors and his quiver of darts. (*Paradiso*, trans. Rabassa,
pp. 238–239)

The project that Lezama proposes for literary criticism is the
study of the intertextual relations that will help to illuminate the
intellectual or artistic stance of each author by means of "retrospective imagination." Though immersed in the pessimism Lezama
sees in Eliot,[21] Harold Bloom proposes something similar in *The
Anxiety of Influence:*

By "poetic influence" I do not mean the transmission of ideas and images from earlier to later poets. This is indeed just "something that happens," and whether such transmission causes anxiety in the later poets
is merely a matter of temperament and circumstances. These are fair
materials for source-hunters and biographers, and have little to do with
my concern. Ideas and images belong to discursiveness and to history,
and are scarcely unique to poetry. *Yet a poet's stance, his Word, his
imaginative identity, his whole being, must* be unique to him, and remain unique, or he will perish, as a poet, if ever even he has managed
his re-birth into poetic incarnation. But this fundamental stance is
as much also his precursor's as any man's fundamental nature is also
his father's, however transformed, however turned about. (p. 71; emphasis added)

In fact, Bloom's phrase "imaginative identity" has a Lezaman ring
to it.
    It is significant that Bloom singles out Goethe (a poet with whom
Lezama strongly identifies) among the few exceptions to the anxiety

of influence. The critic is plainly dismayed at Goethe's optimism: "Nietzsche, as he always insisted, was the heir of Goethe in his strangely optimistic refusal to regard the poetical past as primarily an obstacle to fresh creation. Goethe, like Milton, absorbed precursors with a gusto evidently precluding anxiety" (p. 50). As evidence of Goethe's peculiar status—"Only a poet who believed himself literally incapable of creative anxiety could say this" (p. 51)—Bloom offers the following passage from his autobiography: "It must be that human nature is endowed with a peculiar tenacity and versatility enabling it to overcome everything that it contacts or takes into itself, or, if the thing defies assimilation, at least to render it innocuous" (p. 52). To which Bloom attaches the rejoinder, "This is truer of Goethean than of human nature" (p. 52). I would also add that Goethe's faith in the human capacity for assimilation is also true of Lezaman nature.[22]

Even though Lezama rejects Eliot's critical stance as pessimistic, his thought about the relation between texts in the literary tradition seems deeply affected by Eliot's concept of the retrospective reordering of the tradition by every new text. Lezama's "creative assimilation" also evokes the more current concept of "intertextuality," but it differs from the way that concept is understood by theorists such as Roland Barthes and Julia Kristeva principally because of Lezama's more conservative notion of the sign. The major purpose of the concept of intertextuality and the poststructuralist redefinition of the notion of text is to displace the notion of the subject and of intersubjectivity as the primary relation in literary thought. Despite his methodological radicality, Lezama has no interest in displacing the notion of the subject. Far from it, the philosophical (theological) underpinnings of his poetics depend not only on a concept of the subject but on his faith in the existence of a transcendental subject, God. For Lezama, texts exist as metaphors and are reduced to emblems as if they were figures in a medieval allegory. Lezama's contrapuntal practice of reading invites parallels with the relativism of Barthes and Kristeva, but the parallels fade at the level of their basic philosophical stance: Lezama has no quarrel with humanism.

Chapter 5
. . . .

Textual Epiphany: A Return to Bibliomancy

An "epiphany" is the visible manifestation of a divine (or at least superhuman) being who is considered invisible through ordinary observation. In the strict or full sense of the word it is the manifestation of the person himself; in the less restricted sense it is manifestation of the person only through his effects.
—New Catholic Encyclopedia

Often, for instance, while turning over haphazardly the pages of a book of poetry, one may come upon a line which is extraordinarily appropriate to some matter which is in one's own mind, though the poet himself had no thought of such a thing when he was writing.
—St. Augustine, The Confessions

By an epiphany he meant a sudden spiritual manifestation, whether in the vulgarity of speech or of gesture or in a memorable phase of the mind itself. He believed that it was for the man of letters to record these epiphanies with extreme care, seeing that they themselves are the most delicate and evanescent of moments.
—James Joyce, Stephen Hero

the momentary clarity that is derived from penetrating into quidditary essences.
—José Lezama Lima, "Pascal and Poetry"

. . .

The goal of Lezama's practice of reading is illumination. His essays, as shown in Chapter 4, describe and exemplify the practice of contrapuntal, noncausal reading. *Paradiso* contains passages where this practice is defended by its characters, but the novel also offers something of even greater interest. In a passage of extraordinary audacity and intertextual richness, Lezama conjures up Suetonius, St. Augustine, Goethe, and James Joyce to depict José Cemí's decisive conversion experience.

Nowhere in Lezama's works is the process of poetic epiphany

dramatized with greater detail and intensity than in Cemí's apprenticeship years in *Paradiso*. Although Cemí undergoes a series of poetic experiences throughout his childhood and adolescence: his near-drowning, that of his sister, the game of jacks, his uncle Alberto's letter, and the chess game between his uncles, the illumination he experiences through his reading in Chapter 9 reveals his poetic destiny to him as well as a key to understand human nature. Cemí is prepared for his intertextual illumination by his experience of danger in a bloody confrontation between university students and the mounted police, and an exhortation by his mother, Rialta, to embrace his destiny in life.[1] As told in Chapter 2, Rialta consecrates her son to the danger that will lead to a transfiguration:

> *Pero cuando el hombre, a través de sus días, ha intentado lo más difícil, sabe que ha vivido en peligro, aunque su existencia haya sido silenciosa, aunque la sucesión de su oleaje haya sido manso, sabe que ese día que le ha sido asignado para su transfigurarse, verá, no los peces dentro del fluir, lunarejos en la movilidad, sino los peces en la canasta estelar de la eternidad.* (Obras completas, 1: 321)

· · ·

> But when a man throughout his days has tested what is most difficult, he knows that he has lived in danger, and even though [his] existence has been silent, even though the succession of its waves has been peaceful, he knows that a day has been assigned to him in which he will be transfigured, and he will not see the fish inside the current, dappled in motion, but the fish in the starry basket of eternity. (*Paradiso*, trans. Rabassa, p. 228)

The image of "the starry basket of eternity," which for Lezama represents the ultimate goal of the poetic mission (as well as of life), reappears that very night in Cemí's reading.

The nocturnal reading session is framed not only by the crisis of the young man's first encounter with danger, and his moral decision to risk his life by taking part in the student demonstration, but also by another life-threatening crisis, an attack of asthma. The remarkable events of the day (the student demonstration, the crucial encounter with his friend Fronesis, the emotionally charged conference with his mother, the asthma attack and the therapeutic fumigation of the room) constitute a process of preparation and purification prior to the ritual late-night reading. In a state of high acuity, after a restoring sleep, Cemí returns to the readings he had laid aside at the onset of the asthma attack:

*la amalgama de la algazara, la aparición inesperada de Fronesis y su
acompañante Foción, y sobre todo las palabras de su madre, unido lo
anterior al largo sueño producido por los polvos fumigatorios le pro-
ducían un afán de volver, como en un reencuentro de su sueño con su
circunstancia, a los libros que estaba leyendo. Había abandonado a
Suetonio en el capítulo dedicado a Nerón, al que quería leer en el silen-
cio de la medianoche.* (1: 324)

. . .

The amalgam of the turbulence, Fronesis's unexpected appearance with
his companion Foción, above all, his mother's words, all linked by the
long sleep permitted by the fumes, produced an urge to unite his sleep
and his surroundings, to go back to the books he was reading. He had
left Suetonius in the chapter on Nero, which he wanted to read in the
silence of midnight. (p. 230)

In the first text Cemí chooses to read "in the silence of midnight,"
Suetonius's *Lives of the Caesars,* he discovers the meaning of the
danger mentioned by his mother that leads neither to epiphany nor
to rebirth. The emperor Nero serves as the emblem of the destructive personality: cruel and dazzling, victimizing the weak:

De la primera lectura de esa noche, había saltado la palabra neroniano.
*Era lo que calificaría siempre el desinflamiento de una conducta sin
misterio, lo coruscante, lo cruel, lo preconcebido actuando sobre lo
indefenso, actor espectador, lo que espera en frío que la sombra de la
gaviota pase por su espejo.* (1: 326)

. . .

[From that night's first reading, the word "Neronian" had leaped out.]
For him, this would always mean the detumescence of a conduct without mystery, the biting, cruel, premeditated working on the defenseless,
the spectator-actor, waiting coldly for the shadow of the gull to pass
over its mirror. (p. 231)

Through Cemí's reading the emperor Nero is transformed from a
historical figure into a moral category, "the Neronian."

The other text (or as Lezama calls it "el segundo desfiladero de esa
noche" ["that night's second cliffwalk"], recalling Cortázar's phrase
"lessons about the abyss") that echoes Rialta's words for Cemí is
Goethe's *Wilhelm Meister's Years of Apprenticeship.*[2] In a manner
reminiscent of St. Augustine's conversion, Cemí takes up and reads
a passage in Goethe's *Bildungsroman,* and finds that the text speaks
to him:

Fue buscando los párrafos que había subrayado y de pronto leyó: "A que pocos varones les ha sido otorgado el poder presentarse siempre de modo regulado, lo mismo que los astros, y gobernar tanto el día como la noche, formar sus utensilios domésticos; sembrar y recolectar, conservar y gastar, y recorrer siempre el mismo círculo con calma, amor y acomodación al objeto."³ (1: 326)

. . .

He was looking for the paragraphs he had underlined and suddenly he read: "[How] few men have been awarded the power of always showing themselves in a regulated way, the same as the stars, and governing the day as well as the night, shaping their domestic utensils; sowing and reaping, saving and spending, and passing along the same circle, always with calmness, love, and accommodation to the object." (p. 231)

"Recognizing" himself in the description of the harmonious man given in the passage, Cemí writes in the margin "Me?"—not out of adolescent arrogance, explains the narrator, but out of sincere recognition:

él sabía que era esa alusión a la costumbre de los astros, a su ritmo de eterna seducción creadora, a un Eros que conocía como las estaciones, lo que lo había llevado a esa frase, más con la aceptación de una amorosa confianza, que con la tentación de una luciferina vanidad omnisciente. (1: 326; emphasis added)

. . .

he knew that the reference to *the stars' habits,* to *their rhythm of eternal, creative seduction,* to an Eros that [he knew like] the seasons, had drawn him to that passage, more in the spirit of accepting an amorous confidence than of the temptation of an omniscient, luciferine vanity. (p. 231; emphasis added)

The next day at noon, upon hearing a Ravel quartet, Cemí has an analogous experience. The noontime audition of the quartet echoes the midnight reading; the configurations of the previous night's reading, the opposition between "fluidity" and "fixedness," arise from Cemí's perception of the quartet in terms of the ocean. For the young man the form of the quartet

contenía implícitas la participación y la justificación, así cada compás estaba hecho en relación con la corriente sonora, con su fluencia en persecución de una suprema esencia y al mismo tiempo parecía mirarle la cara con fijeza *a todo el que se le acercaba para dar cuenta de sus actos en el cosmos del sonido.* (1: 328; emphasis added)

· · ·

contained implicit participation and justification, [so that] each rhythm was created in relation to the flow of sound, and its *current pursued a supreme essence, and at the same time it seemed to be staring into the [face]* of everything that came close, and thus it brought about a realization of its acts within the cosmos of sound. (p. 233)

The configurations of the quartet reappear during Cemí's walk through the port of Havana that afternoon, when his imagination responds with a version of the "fixedness of the stars" and the harmonious man described in *Wilhelm Meister:*

Los pargos que oyen estupefactos las risotadas de los motores de las lanchas, los garzones desnudos que ascienden con una moneda en la boca, las reglanas casas de santería con la cornucopia de frutas para calmar a los dioses del trueno, la compenetración entre la fijeza estelar y las incesantes mutaciones de las profundidades marinas, *contribuyen a formar una región dorada para un hombre que resiste todas las posibilidades del azar con una inmensa sabiduría placentera.* (1: 329; emphasis added)

· · ·

The [red snappers] who listen in stupefaction to the ship's motors, the naked young divers who swim up with coins in their mouths, the *santería* temples of Regla with a cornucopia of fruit to calm the gods of thunder, the interpenetration of *the fixedness of the stars and the incessant mutations of the marine depths* that form a gilded zone for a man who can resist all the possibilities of chance with an immense, [serene] wisdom. (p. 233; emphasis added)

This third aesthetic experience joins Goethe's celestial imagery to Cemí's perception of the Ravel quartet in marine terms. Once again the apprentice poet stumbles upon the golden region between the fixedness of the stars (that is, immortality) and the fluidity of the ocean, the region which belongs to the tense equilibrium of poetry.

The danger without epiphany which can lead Cemí astray is incarnated by the character Eugenio Foción, in whom Cemí recognizes a destructive and sterile force.[4] This revelation occurs the afternoon after his decisive midnight readings. The second encounter with Foción (Cemí had met him during the demonstration) provides an occasion to employ his newly found poetic knowledge. Significantly, the scene is literally played out among books, since the incident occurs in a bookstore, where, with characteristic passivity, Cemí witnesses the scene unobserved. In order to play a joke on a naïve acquaintance, Foción asks the owner of the bookstore for a new book: "¿Ya llegó el Goethe de James Joyce, que acaba de publicar en Ginebra?" (1: 329) ("Has James Joyce's *Goethe* come in yet, the one that was just published in Geneva?" [p. 234]), a work the narrator assures us has never been written. Foción's unsuspecting victim is taken in and orders a copy immediately. Cemí, irked by the unpleasant scene, interprets it in terms of his intertextual epiphany:

> Vino al recuerdo de José Cemí su lectura de Suetonio la noche anterior, y precisó que el diálogo de Foción había sido una situación enteramente neroniana. Conocía a su interlocutor, la dolencia que lo exacerbaba; mientras éste estaba indefenso en su poder, él podía permanecer incólume. Podía jugar, mientras la otra persona se irritaba en su enfermedad. Utilizaba su superioridad intelectual, no para ensanchar el mundo de las personas con quienes hablaba, sino para dejar la marca de su persona y de sus caprichos. . . . Partía siempre de su innata superioridad, si se le aceptaba esa superioridad reaccionaba con sutiles descargas de ironía, si por el contrario se la negaban, mostraba entonces una indiferencia de caracol, tan peligrosa como su ironía. Hería con un puñal de dos puntas, ironía e indiferencia, y él siempre permanecía en su centro, lanzando una elegante bocanada de humo. Era el árbitro de las situaciones neronianas. (1: 330–331)

• • •

Cemí recalled his reading of Suetonius the night before and could see that Foción's dialogue had [been] a thoroughly Neronian situation. He had known the person he was talking to and the illness that aggravated him; he remained untouched, while the other one was defenseless in his power. He played with him, while the other became more upset and ill. He did not use his intellectual superiority to [broaden] the world of the people he spoke to, but to score a mark with his personality and his whims. . . . His starting point was always his innate superiority; if that superiority was accepted, he would react with subtle shots of irony; if, on the contrary, it was denied, then he would show a snail-like indifference, just as dangerous as his irony. He wounded with a two-pointed dagger, irony and indifference, and he was always at the center, blowing [out an elegant puff of smoke]. He was the arbiter of Neronian situations. (p. 234–235)

By recognizing Foción as a Neronian character, Cemí affirms his rejection of any danger that leads merely to emptiness and simultaneously defines his poetic mission. In opposition to Foción, he will use

his intellect to broaden the world of those who come into contact
with him. The reading of Suetonius provides the moral category that
characterizes Foción, while the underlined passage from *Wilhelm
Meister* offers a model for Cemí's behavior.

Interestingly, however, despite the assertion of the narrator, it is
clear that "James Joyce's *Goethe*" *does* exist for Lezama, at least,
if not also for Cemí. The intertextual cluster which brings about
Cemí's epiphany provides the key to unscramble the title of Foción's
spurious book. James Joyce's *Goethe,*that is to say, Joyce's *Wilhelm
Meister* is *A Portrait of the Artist as a Young Man.* If Cemí discovers
his mirror image in Goethe's *Wilhelm Meister,* Lezama himself also
finds his in the work of Joyce.

In his essay of 1941, "Muerte de Joyce" ("Joyce's Death"), Lezama
appropriates *Portrait* by describing it in terms of his own poetic system: "Hoy vamos viendo que aquella obra se hizo como se hacen
todas las obras: la lucha adolescente entre el sexo y el dogma, el
ritmo de la voz y cierta heterodoxia superficial que va en busca de
una ortodoxia central" (2: 237). ("Today we see that his work was
made as all other works are made: the adolescent struggle between
sex and dogma, the rhythm of the voice and a certain superficial heterodoxy in search of a central orthodoxy.") Although Lezama does
isolate the elements in Joyce's work that are also central to his own
outlook, his unqualified assimilation of the Irish author's work
obscures fundamental poetical and philosophical differences. The
formula Lezama employs to describe Joyce's ideological stance, a
"superficial heterodoxy in search of a central orthodoxy," is, in fact,
nothing more than a projection onto the Irish author of his own position. Lezama's formula only fits Joyce if it is reversed to read: a "superficial orthodoxy in search of a central heterodoxy." Nothing becomes clearer after an examination of the important concept of the
"epiphany" in the work of Joyce and a comparison with the role that
concept plays in Lezama.

Joyce's concept of the "epiphany," particularly foregrounded in the
early works: *Dubliners, Stephen Hero* (an early version of *Portrait*),
and *A Portrait of the Artist as a Young Man,* has been a major preoccupation for critics over the years. In their study, critics have had
to contend with several obstacles: the distinction between the genre
of epiphanies practiced by Joyce (these could be considered prose
poems that capture a moment of illumination) and the concept of
aesthetic illumination itself, the three-stage evolution of the concept, and the problem of reconciling Joyce's modernist outlook with
the scholastic pedigree he claims for his concept.

Richard Ellmann gives the best summary of the origin and the scope of the term "epiphany":

> Accordingly he [Joyce] began in 1900, and continued until 1903, to write a series of what, because he was following no one, he declined to call prose poems as others would have done. For these he evolved a new and more startling descriptive term, 'epiphanies.' The epiphany did not mean for Joyce the manifestation of godhead, the showing forth of Christ to the Magi, although that is a useful metaphor for what he had in mind. The epiphany was the sudden 'revelation of the whatness of a thing,' the moment in which 'the soul of the commonest object . . . seems to us radiant.' The artist, he felt, was charged with such revelations, and must look for them not among gods but among men, in casual, unostentatious, even unpleasant moments. He might find 'a sudden spiritual manifestation' either 'in vulgarity of speech or of gesture or in a memorable phase of the mind itself.' Sometimes the epiphanies are 'eucharistic,' another term arrogantly borrowed by Joyce from Christianity and invested with secular meaning. These are moments of fullness or of passion. Sometimes the epiphanies are rewarding for another reason, that they convey precisely the flavor of unpalatable experiences. The spirit, as Joyce characteristically held, manifested itself on both levels. They vary also in style: sometimes they read like messages in an unfamiliar tongue; their brilliance lies in their peculiar baldness, their uncompromising refusal of all devices which would render them immediately clear. At other times they are deliberately unenciphered, and lyrically biased.[5]

Ellmann also discusses the relation of certain epiphanies to dreams, and explains that although Freud's *The Interpretation of Dreams* had appeared in 1899, "Joyce's interest in dreams is pre-Freudian in that it looks for revelations, not scientific explanation" (*James Joyce*, p. 85).

Harry Levin focuses especially on the mystical aspect of the epiphany:

> The writer, no longer hoping to comprehend modern life in its chaotic fullness, was searching for external clues to its inner meaning. . . . It follows that the writer, like the mystic, must be peculiarly aware of these manifestations. What seem trivial details to others may be portentous symbols to him. In this light, Joyce's later works are artificial reconstructions of a transcendental view of experience. His dizzying shifts between mystification and exhibitionism, between linguistic experi-

ment and pornographic confession, between myth and autobiography, between symbolism and naturalism, are attempts to create a literary substitute for the revelations of religion.[6]

Levin's conclusion clarifies the distance that separates Lezama from Joyce. The unbelieving Irish author looks upon epiphany as a surrogate for religious revelation. Literary knowledge and religious knowledge are irreconcilable, competing systems for Joyce, while for Lezama they are complementary. Joyce's literary epiphanies substitute a secular mysticism for that of religion. Lezama's literary epiphanies instead purport to be a bridge between art and religion. Joyce's heterodoxy is clear on this score despite Lezama's attempts to assimilate him.

There are, nevertheless, three principal factors that mitigate Lezama's "creative assimilation" of the Joycean concept of epiphany. The Irish and the Cuban writer both share: a view of the epiphany as a moment of grace, a belief in the guiding power of epiphanies, and an essential subjectivism that frequently renders their epiphanies inaccessible to their readers.

Joyce's assimilation of the concept of grace to his secular religion of poetry is a good example of his "superficial orthodoxy and central heterodoxy." As Umberto Eco makes clear, Joyce retains the vocabulary and the framework of Catholicism but employs them for his own ends. Eco is not fooled by the trappings Joyce perversely borrows from Aquinas. Beneath the Thomistic posturing of the Irish novelist he detects a fundamentally romantic notion of poetry and the role of the poet as seer.[7] Eco concludes that the poetics of the romantics and in particular those of their symbolist descendants like Walter Pater and Gabriele D'Annunzio have a more profound effect on Joyce's view of literary creation than the thought of Aquinas despite Stephen Dedalus's famous formulation of his poetics through the Thomistic terms *quidditas, integritas, consonantia,* and *claritas* in *A Portrait of the Artist as a Young Man.*[8] In fact, Eco attributes the origin of the very term "epiphany" to Joyce's reading of D'Annunzio's novel *Il Fuoco (The Flame of Life).*[9]

Perhaps the characteristic subjectivism of the Joycean epiphany is a natural consequence of his essentially romantic aesthetics. There is some disagreement among critics regarding the level of subjectivity of Joyce's epiphanies and to what degree this permits or bars the reader from sharing in the illuminating experience. More optimistic than recent critics, Irene Hendry Chayes sees the issue in terms of Joyce's evolution as a narrator. She posits three distinct epiphany techniques that correspond to *Dubliners, Stephen Hero,* and *A Portrait of the Artist as a Young Man*, and feels that the last one successfully includes the reader.[10] Hélène Cixous is more qualified than Chayes regarding the subjectivism of Joyce's epiphany technique in *Portrait*. For her there are "incoherent moments" when the epiphany is not shared by the reader.[11] Joyce's subjectivism is precisely his crucial departure from the aesthetic philosophy of Aquinas, according to Eco.[12] Eco's analysis of the actual genesis of the Joycean epiphany reveals the essentially subjective nature of these illuminations in comparison to the more objective "moments privilegiés" in Proust. The epiphanies experienced by Stephen Dedalus, Eco maintains, are the product of an internal and thereby nonverifiable process.[13]

Cemí's epiphanic experiences in *Paradiso* are more varied than those of Stephen in *Portrait*. In Lezama, the point of departure for the illuminating moments experienced by the young protagonist is, as in Joyce, most often a common enough, even unsavory occurrence. The manner in which the authors develop their epiphanies is, however, considerably different. Except in the case of what Ellmann calls the dream epiphanies, where according to Cixous's description "the transition to the world of delirium from the ordinary world is made without warning," Joyce usually remains within the bounds of a reality acutely experienced by the poetic sensibility of Stephen.[14] What is the exception in Joyce, however, becomes the norm for Lezama, who departs from a similarly intense observation of reality but soon plunges the reader into a truly delirious perception of the world via an untrammeled succession of extended metaphors, analogies, and images that seem to follow only their own logic.[15] In addition, Cemí is at times subject to phantasmagoric visions more reminiscent of the Circe chapter in *Ulysses* than anything in *Portrait*. Nevertheless, the basic process whereby an otherwise indifferent event acquires an emblematic force for the fledgling poet is shared by Lezama and Joyce.

There is also a close affinity between Joyce and Lezama in the guiding role they accord to epiphanies in the respective apprenticeships of their young poets. Both Cemí and Stephen are guided through the stages of their poetic priesthood by illuminations that occur at crucial moments.[16] Nevertheless, although epiphanies often play an analogous role in *Paradiso* and *Portrait*, they lead in opposite directions. Significantly, one of the epiphanies experienced by Stephen warns him to shun a priestly vocation. The phrasing of the dilemma, the frivolous life symbolized by the song in the street versus the rejection of earthly pleasures evoked by the serious countenance of the man of God, is taken right from the hagiographic tradi-

tion, but Stephen's "wrong" choice constitutes a total inversion of
the archetypal scene whose primary model is the conversion of St.
Augustine to Christianity, and his renunciation of worldly pleasures. In his well-known essay, "The *Portrait* in Perspective," Hugh
Kenner recognizes St. Augustine's *Confessions* as one of the chief
archetypes of Joyce's book.[17] Joyce unquestionably adopts the arche-
type but employs it in such a manner that it subverts the ideological
system it was meant to support.

Unlike Joyce, Lezama adopts not only the structural pattern of the
epiphany but also its traditional ideological content. Lezama's "central orthodoxy" leads him to adapt the model of St. Augustine rather
than subvert it. Stephen Dedalus's luciferine "I will not serve" corre-
sponds, in terms of *Paradiso,* to the stance of Eugenio Foción, not
that of Cemí. Joyce's secularized epiphany, as Harry Levin points
out, is a necessary surrogate given his rejection of religion. The task
Lezama imposes on his protagonist is not the elaboration of a secular religion of poetry but the incorporation of secular poetry into a
vaster religious outlook.

A comparison of Cemí's epiphanic midnight readings to their Augustinian model, the famous "tolle lege" scene in the Milan garden
will clarify the pattern of Lezama's "creative assimilation." In addition, it will demonstrate to what degree Lezama's practice of reading
is indebted to the ancient oracular practice of reading known as
bibliomancy.

It will be remembered that Augustine's decisive conversion, narrated in Book 8, Chapter 12, of the *Confessions,* is precipitated by
his hearing of the words "tolle lege" ("take it and read it"), his interpretation of the voice as a divine command, and his decision that the
book he should take up and read is the very book he had been study-
ing, Paul's epistle to the Romans. The emotional context of these oc-
currences, however, is just as important. Augustine has been prepared to hear the divine command and to receive the words of Paul
"with the ear of the heart" because a series of model conversions referred to him has finally brought him to the threshold of a spiritual
crisis. The last obstacle to his conversion is his acceptance of the life
of chastity recommended by Paul as the most perfect form of Christian living. Flinging himself to the ground, still under the shade of a
fig tree (a symbol of his attachment to the life of the flesh),[18] Augustine pleads for an end to his indecision.[19] In a flash, the random
reading of Romans accomplishes what all the previous poring over
the book had failed to do: Paul's words take root and blossom within
Augustine. Admonished by the randomly chosen passage, as St. Anthony had been by the words of the gospel spoken as he entered a

church, Augustine does not need to read further. He marks the page and refers the experience to his friend, who according to some sort of spiritual chain reaction is in turn "admonished" by the passage that immediately follows the one Augustine had read.

Augustine's random opening of Romans follows a practice of oracular reading that was common to both the Judeo-Christian and the Pagan traditions in antiquity and was known by the names of Sortes Homericae, Sortes Virgilianae, and Sortes Biblicae (respectively: Homeric, Virgilian, and Biblical lots).[20]

Despite his evident ambivalence toward bibliomancy, it is clearly a practice that fascinated Augustine throughout his life. At a time in his life, preceding his conversion to Christianity, when Augustine was interested in becoming an astrologer, a physician friend had used the example of bibliomancy to demonstrate the spuriousness of astrology and other forms of divination.[21] The good physician's advice, nevertheless, fell on deaf ears, for Augustine continued to study astrology for some time and used books as oracles, albeit with variations, throughout his life. The two major concessions Augustine seems to have made after his conversion were to restrict the use to spiritual matters and to employ only the Bible.

Augustine's recourse to Sortes Biblicae contains a paradox. This most subjective of all methods of literary interpretation, where the reader wilfully imposes a context (the reader's own life) on a randomly chosen text, is resorted to as an ultimate attempt to guarantee the objectivity of a decision. Arbitrariness, normally taken to be the hallmark of subjectivism, in the case of the Sortes Biblicae, opens the door to divine intervention. To the mind of the believer, however, there is no paradox; the personal will has been suppressed so that the will of God will manifest itself directly. Robert Meagher sees the "apertio libri" as Augustine's attempt to banish willfulness from his conversion.[22]

Through his decision to interpret the voice of a child chanting "take it and read it" as a divine command to apply the Sortes Biblicae to Paul's epistle, Augustine seeks to approach the conversions of his models: St. Anthony, Victorinus, and the friends of Ponticianus who were converted by reading the life of St. Anthony. But Augustine's account of his conversion is also motivated by the more dramatic conversion of his principal model, Paul, who on his way to persecute Christians in Damascus, was hurled from his horse, blinded by a heavenly light and heard the voice of Christ (Acts 9:1–9). Unlike Augustine's conversion, Paul's leaves no room for interpretation. Augustine concludes that since he knows of no game in which children call out "take up and read," the voice must be divine, and he must further interpret that command: "being quite certain that I must interpret this as a divine command to me to open the book and read the first passage which I should come upon." How different from the unambiguous account of Acts, where the voice speaking to Paul identifies itself as that of Jesus.

Augustine yearns for the voice of truth, the voice of Jesus, to speak to him as it did to Paul, but he is left to interpret like St. Anthony. Significantly, Meagher notes the stress on "hearing" and "seeing" found in Augustine's writings, but particularly in the account of his conversion.[23]

Meagher's description of the mystical moment of Augustine's conversion embraces the principal formulations of Joyce and Lezama. Seizing the whatness, the *quidditas,* is for Joyce the essence of any epiphanic experience and by extension the principal mystical exercise of his secular religion of poetry. Being held still ("la fijeza" ["fixedness"]) is the ultimate desideratum of Lezama's mystical poetics.

In Joyce there is an analogous valorization of stasis, but exclusively for aesthetic reasons and totally devoid of religious transcendence.[24] Lezama's well-known aesthetic and ethical valorization of "la fijeza" (fixedness) and its pythagorean variation, the hesychastic rhythm achieved by Cemí at the end of the novel, reflect, as Meagher says, the "splendor of eternity which is forever still" experienced during ecstasy. In this context the meaning of the sibyline words of Cemí's mother becomes clearer. According to Rialta, the person who achieves "transfiguration" (ecstasy, revelation) "will not see the fish inside the current but the fish in the starry basket of eternity" (p. 228). The assignation of a negative value to fluidity and a positive value to stasis now becomes comprehensible.

Strictly speaking Cemí's nocturnal reading session is not an initial *apertio libri* (was Augustine's?) but a purposeful return to a marked text and an acceptance of the pertinence of its message to the life of the reader. The young poet's epiphanic reading, nonetheless, partakes of the arbitrariness of bibliomancy and is cast in the pattern of Augustine's conversion. Like the episode in the Milan garden, it is preceded by emotional turmoil: Cemí's encounter with danger, the emotional homecoming, and the resulting asthma attack act as a catharsis that purifies the young man and prepares him for the revelations he will find in his purposeful, random reading. Cemí's crisis of breathing parallels Augustine's spiritual crisis, and a restoring sleep brings it to an end just as the child's voice frees Augustine from his convulsive weeping. Both return to books they had been attempting to read but which their respective crises prevented them from penetrating. They read at random and in silence: Cemí wants to read Suetonius's chapter on Nero in "the silence of midnight," and Augustine's reading is also silent, a rare custom in his day and a sign of intense concentration. Commentators of the *Confessions* have seen in Augustine's silent reading an imitation of another of his models, St. Ambrose, who like Cicero was admired for this remarkable ability.[25] Further similarities include the fact that neither reads further after finding the pertinent passage and that both passages (the one in Romans and the one in *Wilhelm Meister*) provide a program for leading one's life.

Cemí's textual epiphany, which must be considered a crucial conversion to his ethical and poetic mission since it defines him vis-à-vis Foción, the force of self-destruction and sterility, depends on Lezama's practice of contrapuntal reading discussed in the previous chapter. The textual passages are lifted from their contexts and applied to the existential context of the reader. Lezama's selection of a passage from *Wilhelm Meister* for the epiphanic reading that will strengthen Cemí's resolve to pursue a poetic career reveals the conscious arbitrariness of his practice of reading. Cemí's ultimate choice of a vocation directly contradicts that of his model, Wilhelm Meister, who at the end of the novel rejects his artistic mission. Breon Mitchell has commented on Wilhelm's unexpected rejection of the artistic life and has argued that in a sense *A Portrait* attempts to correct Wilhelm's wrong choice.[26] Joyce subverts Goethe's archetypal *Bildungsroman* by having the protagonist of his novel of education reach the opposite conclusion from his German forebear. Lezama goes one step further by arbitrarily enlisting Goethe's words against his will.

Furthermore, the passage Cemí marks in *Wilhelm Meister* has nothing to do with the protagonist of the novel. In Book 7, Chapter 6, Wilhelm merely listens to Theresa's account of her life and her frustrated love for Lothario. The words quoted by Lezama are spoken by Lothario during a conversation about the role of men and women in society which Theresa, who was present, refers to Wilhelm. In response to the argument put forth by several ladies that men deprive women of an education in higher culture in order to keep them as playthings or housekeepers, Lothario explains that it is in fact men who are at a disadvantage. Stressing the importance of household management, Lothario explains that women can more easily achieve harmony in their lives by presiding over the harmony of the household. Men, on the other hand, must strive in the moral chaos of the external world and thereby forfeit the "highest ambition," harmony with themselves. It is at that point that Lothario exclaims, "How few men are in a position where they can return regularly like a star, so to speak, and preside both over day and night! Or design their own domestic implements, plant and reap, save and spend, and always move in their orbit with calm, love and a sense of purpose!" (*Wilhelm Meister*, trans. Waidson, 3: 32). This description of man's highest ambition serves as one of the textual sites for Cemí's epiphany. Its astral imagery is borrowed by Lezama again and again to express the desired pattern of life.

The only logical link between *The Lives of the Caesars* and *Wilhelm Meister* is the consciousness of Cemí. In his character's mind Lezama dramatizes an unlikely dialogue between Suetonius and Goethe that not only makes sense, but gives a sense of direction to the fledgling poet. The intertextual dialogue establishes the parameters for the young poet's conduct: Nero (identified with Foción) represents the perversion of art and intelligence for the gratification of the ego, while the harmonious man described in the passage from Goethe not only becomes the model Cemí will seek to follow but is taken by the young man to be a sort of prophecy of his destiny.

By applying an epiphanic text to himself, Cemí, like St. Anthony and St. Augustine, is "admonished" and chooses a special course in life. Stephen Dedalus too was admonished by an epiphany to choose a special vocation, but the vocation of poetry for Joyce unequivocably supplants religion. The Joycean epiphany is divested of religious transcendence. Lezama's synthetic strategy (he would have said "American") embraces both the Joycean application of the epiphanic experience to the secular vocation of poetry and the traditional religious transcendence of the epiphanic experience as known by the Church Fathers.

Lezama's idiosyncratic stance as a believing Christian and literary modernist allows him to perform a feat unthinkable in any other modernist. The Cuban writer accepts the notion of the secular vocation of art originally propounded by the symbolists and canonized by modernists such as Joyce and Proust. But while "the religion of art" originally served as a stopgap to fill the Nietzschean death of God and the fearsome abyss of Mallarmé's blank page, in Lezama it does not set itself up as a rival ideology to religion. Working within the bounds of modernism, Lezama nevertheless returns art to its medieval function as a harmonious component of the Christian path to salvation. Lezama appropriates the works of Joyce, Mallarmé, and Proust, but those of St. Augustine and St. Thomas Aquinas are never far from his consciousness.

Chapter 6
· · · · · · ·

Conclusion: The Henri Rousseau of the Latin American Boom

*Perhaps even here they will regard me as a child
—it can't be helped! For some reason everyone
regards me as an idiot, too. . . . But what sort
of an idiot am I now when I know myself that people
take me for an idiot!*
—Dostoevsky, The Idiot

*"Only bad faith could lead one to believe that the man
capable of suggesting such ideas to us is a bad artist."*
—Early review of Henri Rousseau's work

· · ·

Is José Lezama Lima a primitive or a primitivist? Is the essential idiosyncracy of his style and his outlook a result of the naïveté of a self-taught man of letters or a sign of his radical originality? Is that original style truly due to intention or merely a consequence of his defective technique? Finally, is this Cuban colossus the seminal Latin American writer of the second half of the twentieth century or an elaborate hoax perpetrated on the reading public by the sophisticated public relations machinery of the leading writers and critics of the Latin American Boom?

These questions and the essential problem of Lezama as a literary phenomenon recall a similar problem that arose in the plastic arts at the beginning of the century. The case of the discovery of Henri Rousseau by the avant-garde painters and art dealers of pre–World War I Paris presents numerous parallels with the discovery of Lezama by an analogous group, the writers and critics of the Latin American Boom. The parallel is particularly suggestive because Lezama himself was deeply interested in Rousseau. The poet Guillaume Apollinaire, the writer Alfred Jarry, the painters Pablo Picasso, Georges Braque, Robert Delaunay and Max Weber, and the art dealer Wilhelm Uhde discovered and enthroned Henri Rousseau as a model for modern art. Likewise, Lezama was "discovered" (after more than thirty years of writing poetry and essays and publishing *Orígenes*, one of the most remarkable art journals in Latin America) by Julio Cortázar, Mario Vargas Llosa, and the critic Emir Rodríguez Monegal, among others, promoted to the pantheon occupied by Octavio Paz

and Jorge Luis Borges (by Cortázar), and his work described as among
the most decisive of the century (by Rodríguez Monegal).[1]

In the realm of aesthetic evaluation, like Lezama, Rousseau presents certain problems that embarrass even his most ardent adherents. Thus the young American painter Max Weber, who revered
the older painter as a spiritual father, could not help feeling ill at
ease when he invited Picasso to meet Rousseau:

> Arriving at Rousseau's studio, they [Picasso and Weber] found Apolli-
> naire posing for the first version of *The Muse Inspiring the Poet.* . . .
> Weber states that ". . . for Picasso, it was a new and an all-absorbing and
> enchanting experience. He leaned over and watched every stroke of his
> brush. . . ." At one point, Weber noticed that the arm of the "Muse" was
> about the same length as her body. He whispered to Picasso, "Do you
> think that the left hand will stay that long?" Picasso smiled, shrugged
> and replied, "Je ne sais pas."[2]

Although it apparently did not disturb Picasso, who was absorbed in
watching Rousseau's technique, the "Muse's" overlong arm was a
stumbling block for Weber. Similarly, Lezama's notorious misspell-
ing of foreign proper names, inventive erudition, and macaronic
Greek and Latin have been noted sympathetically by his self-styled
disciple Severo Sarduy:

> To speak of Lezama's errors—even if it is to say that they are not im-
> portant—is *already* not to have read him. If his history, his archeology,
> his aesthetics are delirious, if his Latin is laughable, if his French is like
> the nightmare of a Marseilles typographer, and for his German it is
> futile to exhaust all dictionaries, it is because on the Lezaman page
> what counts is not the veracity—in the sense of identity with some-
> thing nonverbal—of the word, but its *dialogical presence*, its glitter.
> What counts is the texture *French, Latin, culture*, the chromatic value,
> the level they signify in the vertical cut of the writing, in its unfurling
> of parallel wisdom.[3]

Other critics have seen these aspects of Lezama's work purely as
symptoms of cultural underdevelopment. Julio Rodríguez-Luis sees
Paradiso largely as the grotesque failure of a gifted but haphazardly
educated writer.[4] Rodríguez-Luis feels that Lezama deserves praise
for providing an artistic model for several generations of Cuban artists, but despite his valiant efforts to transcend the conditions under
which he worked, in the final analysis, Lezama falls victim to the
realities of socioeconomic and cultural underdevelopment. Horst

Rogmann, who rejects Sarduy's response as an attempt to make a virtue out of a vice, believes that *Paradiso* hurts rather than helps the cause of Latin American letters because of its unreliable erudition.[5] Curiously enough, these two critics and Sarduy are fundamentally in agreement when it comes to the description of Lezama's writing, but they diverge radically when it comes to its evaluation. Judging according to the standards of a European tradition that springs from Descartes, it is logical for Rogmann to suggest that Lezama cannot be considered the equal of European rationalist writers, much less their superior. The principal difference in these antagonistic readings of Lezama is that Sarduy, unlike these critics, does not assume that Lezama wants to play the game of European culture as a European.

Ultimately the crucial question before the reader of Lezama and the viewer of Rousseau's paintings is the same one: Did they fail to master the rudiments of artistic systems that they admired (European novelistic realism and the realism of French academic painting, respectively) and unwittingly produce caricatures, or did they chart a path into the unknown? And before the unknown there are always two reactions. The most common one, diffidence (and fear?), is exemplified by the comment of a critic who viewed a small collection of Rousseau paintings at the first one-man exhibition ever held of his work. The critic, Elizabeth Luther Carey, put her predicament very candidly: "our mind must rebel a bit at such a leap as he asks us to take into the unknown."[6] A rarer response, wholehearted acceptance, is that of Julio Cortázar, who upon first reading *Paradiso*, praised Lezama for developing a narrative system not born of books but of "long lessons at and about the abyss."[7]

Before tracing further the analogy between the Cuban writer and the French painter and seeing what Lezama has to say about him, which is much and of great interest, it is necessary to review the essentials of the case of Henri Rousseau. For this purpose, Roger Shattuck's study in *The Banquet Years* is still the best source.

There are primarily three readings of Henri Rousseau as person and artist. The first, which largely feeds on the anecdotes narrated by Guillaume Apollinaire, whom Shattuck has called "less a biographer than an unexcelled forger of myth" (p. 45), and Wilhelm Uhde (Rousseau's first biographer), posits a totally naïve man who was the constant target of practical jokes, even at the hands of his friends. Some of these jokes were rather cruel and consisted in making Rousseau believe that he was achieving the official recognition (from famous academic painters, the President of France, etc.) that he so much desired and expected. Others exploited the painter's

Conclusion

particular idiosyncracies, such as his belief in ghosts. Shattuck sums
up an episode that has become an integral part of the legend of "le
Douanier":[8]

> According to Apollinaire and Wilhelm Uhde, a dealer-critic in Paris and
> later a good friend of the painter, Rousseau believed in ghosts and spir-
> its. He encountered them during his long watches in remote places and
> told the other *gabelous* how, when the ghosts mocked him with foul
> smells, he shot at them. His fellow workers rigged up a false ghost on
> strings between wine barrels; Rousseau confounded them by doffing his
> hat and asking if it would have a drink. These stories, even if apoc-
> ryphal, indicate that his victimization as a naïf began before his artistic
> pretensions took shape. (p. 48)

Although Apollinaire and Uhde must be credited with the recognition of Rousseau's worth as an artist, and Uhde helped materially
by acting as his art dealer, they are also responsible for the legend of
"le Douanier." From other unimpeachable evidence, it is indisput-
able that Rousseau was an exceptionally ingenuous person in his
daily life. Nevertheless, even if many of Apollinaire's and Uhde's anecdotes are true, they establish a strong link between Rousseau the
person and the artist that deformed the evaluation of his work for a
long time.

The second reading of Rousseau, though antagonistic to that of
Apollinaire and Uhde, in fact derives its major premise from their
exaggerated emphasis on the artist's naïveté. Basing himself on evidence of Rousseau's capacity to appraise correctly his better works,
Charles Chassé (as cited by Shattuck) rejected his alleged ingenuousness and argued that Rousseau was in fact a hoax who "really duped
friends and enemies alike and made a name for himself through
a highly knowledgeable fraud on public taste."[9] The third reading,
advanced by Shattuck, strikes a balance between the extremes of
Rousseau the total innocent and the hoax: "Rousseau, a true artisan,
painted with a combination of insight and awkwardness that has
earned him double standing as both modern and primitive artist"
(p. 30).

Without minimizing Rousseau's personal ingenuousness and the
primitive aspects of his painting, Shattuck makes a strong case for
Rousseau's consciousness of his method and his devotion to the perspective of the "child-man." For Shattuck it is this personal "primitivism," this search for a valuable, lost past that explains the attrac-
tion Rousseau exerted on the painters of the avant-garde, who also

Henri Rousseau, *The Dream* (1910). Oil on canvas, 6'8 1/2" × 9'9 1/2". Collection, The Museum of Modern Art, New York. Gift of Nelson A. Rockefeller.

prized those traits in African art.[10] As one of Rousseau's last letters makes clear, it is a perspective he never abandoned. In that letter, the painter answers critic André Dupont's inquiry regarding the presence of a sofa in the middle of the jungle in the painting *The Dream*. Rousseau's explanation is very simple: "This woman sleeping on this sofa dreams that she is transported in the middle of this forest, hearing the notes of the charmer's pipe."[11] But Rousseau adds a brief comment that is a manifesto in itself:

if I have kept my naïveté, it is because M. Gérôme, who was a professor at the Beaux-Arts, as well as M. Clément, director of Beaux-Arts at the Ecole de Lyon, always told me to keep it. You will no longer find that amazing in the future. And I have been told before that I was not of this century. I will not now be able to change my manner which I have acquired by stubborn application, believe me.[12]

Rousseau isolates his naïveté as the key component of his manner, and he is not only conscious but proud of it, since he perceives that it opens the door to the art of the future. Remarkable as this statement is, it fails to articulate a truly revolutionary explanation of the presence of the red sofa that Rousseau offered André Salmon, "You shouldn't be surprised to find a sofa out in a virgin forest. It means nothing except for the richness of the red."[13] Rousseau's rejection of the principle of verisimilitude in favor of a new value, the visual impact caused by the juxtaposition of the red velvet couch and the jungle, recalls Sarduy's explanation of Lezama's style as a rejection of verisimilitude and veracity. For Rousseau and for Lezama what counts is not the reference of what they respectively paint and write to a reality, but (to use Sarduy's words) "the texture," "the chromatic value" of what is offered on the canvas or on the page. The unexpected juxtapositions of Henri Rousseau (the couch and the jungle in *The Dream*, the gypsy and the lion in *The Sleeping Gypsy*, the well-dressed lady with her parasol in the middle of the forest in *Walking in the Forest*, the figures in carnival costume set against a wintry forest in *A Carnival Evening*) like those of Lezama create an aura of mystery as they strive for a truth different than that made possible by the conventions of pictorial or narrative realism.

The reception of the works of Lezama also parallels that of Henri Rousseau. Both artists worked in obscurity until they were discovered and thrust to the forefront of the most important cultural movement of their time. Although the parallel is valid, it is so only up to a point. Lezama was never a "Sunday poet," and whatever jobs he held had only one function as far as he was concerned, to allow him to live in order to create. Rousseau came to a full-time artist's career at the age of forty when he retired from the river toll service, while Lezama's career can be considered launched from the time of the publication of his first poem, "Muerte de Narciso" ("Death of Narcissus"), in 1937 when he was twenty-six.[14] That same year, a landmark one for Lezama, he published several issues of his first literary journal, *Verbum* (a publication of the law students at the University of Havana), his interview with Juan Ramón Jiménez, "Coloquio con Juan Ramón Jiménez" ("Colloquy with Juan Ramón Jiménez") appeared, and he received the encouragement and friendship of the famous poet.[15] Before reaching the age of thirty, Lezama had already forged a distinctive style which would not evolve appreciably during the next thirty-nine years, and had begun to assume a position of artistic leadership that would culminate during the years of the publication of his most important journal, *Orígenes* (1944–1956). During those two decades Lezama was the undisputed leader of a small group of poets, novelists, painters, and composers that has come to be known as the *Orígenes* group. Although many of them called Lezama "maestro," they certainly did not seek to imitate his style and were primarily disciples in that they followed his attitude of serious work and complete devotion to the arts.[16]

The demise of *Orígenes* in 1956, brought on by a quarrel between Lezama and José Rodríguez Feo, who had supported the journal financially for many years, signaled the emergence of a new generation known as the *Ciclón* group, after the new journal founded by Rodríguez Feo. Although at the time this new group of writers saw a great difference between themselves and the *Orígenes* writers, with the perspective of time it is easier to see their debt to their predecessors. Although dethroned, Lezama still was an influence to be reckoned with, and they continued to pay him homage by parodying him, as Guillermo Cabrera Infante did in *Tres tristes tigres* (*Three Trapped Tigers*), or as Severo Sarduy has done by imitating and developing his notions of literature.[17]

Three years after the demise of *Orígenes*, the overthrow of Batista and the triumph of the Revolution held out the promise of a new beginning for Cuba's artists as well as for all Cubans. There followed a honeymoon period when different generations of artists published together in *Lunes de Revolución*, the literary supplement of the 26 of July Movement's newspaper *Revolución*. Lezama supported the Revolution and published essays that evinced his hopes for a new Cuba.[18] The event that was to lead to Lezama's worldwide recognition also took place under the auspices of the Revolution. The publication of *Paradiso*, which encountered numerous obstacles and was finally carried out in a small edition, immediately created a furor in Cuba. Whatever the agents and their motivations, the publication of the first edition was stopped and then resumed by the Cuban government. This event and the role of foreign public opinion on the regime's decision to lift the ban on the distribution of the novel has been hotly debated. At the 1982 "International Colloquium on José Lezama Lima's Work" held at Poitiers, Armando Alvarez Bravo stressed the censorship of the novel by Castro's regime.[19] Cintio Vitier's response flatly dismissed Alvarez Bravo's interpretation.[20]

Although the Revolution provided Lezama with ample opportunities to publish his essays and poetry without financial concerns and published his masterpiece (albeit reluctantly), Lezama's worldwide recognition and his contact with the outside world were hampered by Cuba's isolation. The embargo placed on Cuba by the United States and the Organization of American States isolated the island

culturally as well as economically from its Latin American neigh-
bors. Thus political events and the small size of the first edition of
Paradiso conspired against the writer's recognition in the Spanish-
speaking world, where Lezama, with rare exceptions, went unread.
Later, in the 1970's when *Paradiso* was readily available in several
Spanish and Latin American editions and had been translated into
the major European languages, Lezama was unable to savor his success because, although he accepted several invitations to travel
abroad and attend conferences held in his honor, the Cuban government did not allow him to leave the island.[21]

Lezama, however, was fortunate to find a friend who enjoyed great
prestige both in Cuba and abroad and who espoused his cause with
singular zeal. To put it in terms of Henri Rousseau's biography,
Lezama found his Apollinaire, Jarry, Picasso, and Uhde all rolled into
one in the person of Julio Cortázar. The Argentinian writer first
learned of the Cuban author in 1957 through a chance meeting with
Ricardo Vigón, a friend of Lezama's immortalized in *Paradiso* as the
character Ricardo Fronesis. Cortázar recalled that meeting and how
he came to know Lezama in "Encuentros con Lezama Lima" ("En-
counters with Lezama Lima"):

> Embarrassed, I admitted my ignorance, and Vigón returned the follow-
> ing day with an issue of the journal *Orígenes.* That night I became ac-
> quainted with Lezama Lima in one of his most admirable texts, which
> in the journal was entitled *Oppiano Licario* and today is the fourteenth
> and final chapter of *Paradiso.* . . . Seldom have I known how to write to
> those I admire, but I felt that I should tell Lezama that his text had
> given me access to a fabulous realm of literature, and, although I don't
> know how I did it, a month later I received a letter and a package of
> books; among them was *Tratados en La Habana* [*Treatises in Havana*]
> with an almost incredible inscription: "To Julio Cortázar, for his bold
> piercing of the wide wall."
>
> Four years passed during which Lezama and I exchanged letters and
> books. . . . The revolution came and I traveled to Cuba toward the end
> of 1961, fearful as always on the eve of coming face to face with some-
> one I had long awaited and loved. The painter Mariano brought us to-
> gether in a dinner that was particularly exquisite at that moment when
> everything was scarce in Cuba, and Lezama arrived with an appetite
> never refuted from soup to dessert. When I saw him savor the fish and
> drink his wine like an alchemist who observes a precious liquor in his
> vial, I felt what later *Paradiso* would so fully give me: the dazzle of a
> poetry capable of embracing not only the splendor of the word but of the
> totality of life from the most insignificant fiber to cosmic immensity.[22]

In 1966 Lezama sent Cortázar a copy of the first Cuban edition of *Paradiso* with a dedication that affectionately describes their friendship and the affinities that bound them together:

> For my dear friend Julio Cortázar, the same day that I received your magnificent *Hopscotch,* I send you my *Paradiso.* Between you and me there is a very great affection, although we have barely known each other. Sometimes I attribute it to our common Basque ancestor, but at other times it seems to me as if both of us had studied in the same school, or lived in the same neighborhood, or that when one of us sleeps the other keeps watch and reads under a good star.[23]

Cortázar, as is well known, became one of the foremost defenders of *Paradiso* in Cuba as well as its most vocal disseminator and defender abroad. In a sense, he even became its "curator" when it was published by Era in Mexico.[24] In "Encuentros con Lezama Lima" Cortázar also refers to the difficulties *Paradiso* encountered in Cuba when it was published. Cortázar relates that even as he read *Paradiso* in the South of France, "as one who enters into a hallucination that does not deprive him of lucidity, perhaps as Dante when he found himself descending to Hell led by the hand of Virgil" (p. 15), in Cuba:

> Lezama's novel, together with other books and other persons, was falling into a different hell, this time a bureaucratic one from which it would take a long time to issue. Resentment, ignorance, and envy raised their triple head to invent an idiotic Cerberus that barked allegedly revolutionary slogans. Accused of immorality and pornography, *Paradiso* was entering a kind of clandestineness from which it would emerge more brilliant and revolutionary than ever as soon as those truly in charge of culture, Fidel Castro above all, would right the rudder of that ship which had been on the verge of sinking into mediocrity and conformism. It is said that when Fidel was questioned on the steps of the University by students who did not understand why the sale of *Paradiso* had been suspended, he answered that he didn't understand much of what went on in that novel, but that in no way did he think it was counterrevolutionary, an opinion that did not escape the ears of those who accompanied him. And even if I digress a bit, the anecdote significantly coincides with an opinion of Gierek, the Polish leader of the seventies, when he learned that young readers demanded a second edition of *Hopscotch* at a time when second editions were not authorized, apparently in order to save paper. On that occasion Gierek asked to see the book, and he returned it saying: "I don't understand anything, but if the

readers like it, let it be printed again." I forgot to tell it to Lezama the
last time we saw each other and it's a shame because undoubtedly he
would have remembered his dedication in which he so generously joined
our paths. (p. 15)

Whatever may be the truth behind the anecdote narrated by
Cortázar in which Fidel, against the symbolic backdrop of the famous university steps, plays the role of a "deus ex machina," the
fact is that *Paradiso* was distributed in Cuba. The novel and its
author, however, continued to draw fire from the quarters that
Cortázar labels "conformist and mediocre." In response to these attacks and to the obstacles the embargo placed on the worldwide recognition he felt Lezama deserved, Cortázar wrote the essay, "Para
llegar a Lezama Lima," ("To Reach Lezama Lima"), an admirable and
extremely complex document of the friendship between these two
important writers.

It is difficult to estimate the impact of the essay in Cuba. Although the fervent praise of Julio Cortázar, an internationally
known literary figure and an outspoken supporter of the Revolution,
must have worked in Lezama's favor, the end result was not the unqualified triumph the Argentinian writer describes in his essay of
1983. Despite Cortázar's rose-colored view, neither Fidel nor the
leaders of the Cuban literary scene righted the course of the ship of
the Cuban bureaucracy away from conformism and mediocrity, nor
was it possible for Cortázar, his eloquence and zeal notwithstanding,
to convince a Marxist government of the contributions of *Paradiso*
to the revolutionary cause. Lezama's revolutionary poetics would be
appreciated only outside of Cuba by writers such as Cortázar and
Severo Sarduy. If the memory of Lezama has been allowed to survive
in Cuba, it has been largely through a campaign that focuses on his
support of the Revolution and not on an acceptance of his poetics
and worldview. Despite the admirable (and understandable) acrobatics of some of the members of the *Orígenes* group who still live
in Cuba, Lezama's work is irreconcilable with Marxist aesthetics
and ethics.[25]

Outside of Cuba, however, the vast impact of Cortázar's essay cannot be doubted. In it Cortázar placed all of his considerable prestige
on the line in order to bring the world's attention to a literary phenomenon he felt had been unjustly ignored for too long. In his crusade
he was joined by Mario Vargas Llosa, and the Uruguayan critic Emir
Rodríguez Monegal, to whom so many contemporary Latin American authors owe so much. The ultimate result of Cortázar's gen-

erous sponsorship of Lezama was the acceptance of *Paradiso* into the canon of the major novels of the Latin American Boom. With that acceptance came the translations into English, French, German, and Italian, and it is not insignificant that the English translation was done by the translator of the Boom, Gregory Rabassa, who had already brought the major novels of Cortázar, Gabriel García Márquez, and Mario Vargas Llosa to a warmly receptive North American public.

Cortázar's behavior toward Lezama was never stained by the condescendence that often marred Apollinaire's relationship with Henri Rousseau, but rather was characterized by a willingness to accept Lezama as a peer or even as his superior. Thus, although Cortázar can never be accused of patronizing his Cuban find, he cannot be exonerated as easily from the charge of myth-making that Shattuck levels at Apollinaire. Cortázar's myth-making, however, never seeks to victimize Lezama. Furthermore, it is unconscious and derives precisely from his identification with the Cuban writer. The discovery of Lezama is of major personal importance to Cortázar because it entails the discovery of an alter ego.

In Cortázar's work there is a lasting preoccupation with the conflict between American and European worldviews. "El ídolo de las Cícladas" ("The Idol of the Cyclades")[26] contains his clearest exposition of the conflict between the sophisticated, world-weary, cynical European represented by a Parisian couple, the Morands, and the innocent, enthusiastic, primal American embodied by Somoza, the sculptor from the River Plate region. The archeologist Morand and the artist Somoza seek to understand the Cycladic statuette they have found by opposing paths of the mind and the senses respectively. In the end the irrationalism of the Latin American triumphs over the rationalism of the Parisians. Although Somoza is killed by Morand, that very act marks the victory of irrationalism. As the story ends, the Parisian, stripped like a savage, licking the blood-stained stone ax with which he dispatched Somoza, crouches in ambush behind the door, ready to kill his wife, Thérèse, whose wonted punctuality (a trait Cortázar associates with rationality) ironically makes her a victim. In *Hopscotch* that same dichotomy is captured in one character, Horacio Oliveira, who longs to rid himself of the ballast of his European education and sees his rationalism (and his very tendency to think in terms of neat dichotomies) as a disease. Oliveira searches endlessly for "bridges" (La Maga, sadism, jazz, and coprophilia are among them)[27] that will connect him to "the other side of things," but he invariably destroys them.

Horacio Oliveira is clearly not Cortázar's self-portrait, but a study of the Argentinian author's works reveals that the issue that haunts the protagonist of *Hopscotch*, which is rehearsed in the vein of black humor in "The Idol of the Cyclades," was of primary importance to Cortázar.

In Lezama, Cortázar finds such a bridge to "the other side of things." As Cortázar himself says, explaining why he first felt the need to write to an author he had never met, "I felt that I should tell Lezama that his text had given me access to a fabulous realm of literature."[28] What Cortázar valued most was precisely Lezama's ability to dissolve dichotomies and to embrace the totality of existence: "*Paradiso* would so fully give me: the dazzle of a poetry capable of embracing not only the splendor of the word but of the totality of life from the most insignificant fiber to cosmic immensity."[29]

Cortázar's "To Reach Lezama Lima" presents a portrait of the Cuban writer as a primitive artist living in a state of creative grace. And Cortázar feels the need to explain and defend what he considers Lezama's most important characteristic, his American ingenuousness, from the attack of European ironists:

> The defensive irony founded on superficial mistakes is joined by the irony elicited from many readers by the unusual naïveté that surfaces at so many points of Lezama's narrative. In the end, it is out of love for that naïveté that I speak of him here. Beyond any scholarly canon, I know of his penetrating efficacy; while so many search, Parsifal finds, while so many speak, Myshkin knows. The baroque style of complex roots which in our America is yielding products as dissimilar and at the same time as fraternal . . . in the very special case of Lezama is tinted with an aura for which I only find that approximating word: naïveté. An American naïveté, insular in a direct and broad sense, an American innocence. A naïve American innocence, Eleatically, Orphically, opening its eyes at the very beginning of creation. Lezama—Adam prior to the fall. . . . A primitive who knows all, an accomplished *Sorbonnard*, but an American one in the sense that the dried albatrosses of Ecclesiastes have not made him "a wiser and a sadder man" but rather one whose science is palingenesis, what is known is original, jubilant, born like water with Thales and fire with Empedocles. (pp. 52–54)

In order to characterize Lezama's naïveté, Cortázar compares him repeatedly to "the noble savage," to Henri Rousseau, and to the protagonist of Dostoevsky's *The Idiot*, Prince Myshkin. Lezama emerges from these comparisons as a type of wise fool, who can be ridiculed only at the peril of losing vital insights.

Both his incredible superabundance and his lacks originate in that innocent freedom, that free innocence. At times, reading *Paradiso,* one has
an extraterrestrial impression: How is it possible to be unaware of or to
defy to such a degree the taboos of knowledge, the "thus, thou shalt not
write" of our shameful professional commandments? When the innocent American shows himself, the noble savage who treasures the beads
without suspecting that they are worthless, or no longer in style, then
two things can happen with Lezama. One, the one that counts: his ge-
nius bursts through with the primordial strength of the stealer of fire
without the inferiority complexes that weigh so much on us in Latin
America. The other, which makes those who suffer from complexes, the
impeccably cultured, smile, is the Douanier Rousseau side, the embar-
rassing, Myshkin side, the man who in *Paradiso,* after an extraordinary
passage, starts a new paragraph and says with the most absolute tranquillity: "What was the young Ricardo Fronesis doing while his family
history was being recounted?" (pp. 56–57)

Cortázar maintains a double perspective throughout "To Reach
Lezama Lima." He assumes the viewpoint of the "impeccably cultured" in order to forestall intellectual resistance to a work that vio-
lates the taboos of the writing profession and prevent its easy dis-
missal, but he also presents a viewpoint that seeks to proselytize by
virtue of its enthusiastic approval. The choice of the double perspective, however, is not merely rhetorical but once more reproduces a
lifelong conflict. In Cortázar there is a yearning for a primitivistic
view of the world that is ever in conflict with his excellent education. It is not at all difficult for Cortázar to anticipate the attacks of
the "impeccably cultured," since he himself is one of them. Cortázar is simultaneously attracted and embarrassed by Lezama's literary *gaffes.* He defends the cultural mistakes, but feels the need to
correct them in a new edition of the novel to which Lezama significantly gives his wholehearted approval but in which he prefers to
give Cortázar carte blanche rather than to participate actively.[30]
Ultimately Cortázar's reading of Lezama as an ingenuous American adds a fascinating chapter to the five-centuries-old tradition of
European utopianism with regard to America, and we must remember that some of the best practitioners of the myth of the noble savage (James Fenimore Cooper, and Alejo Carpentier to name but two)
have been Americans with European eyes. Cortázar's "ingenuous,
innocent" Lezama is as much a myth as Apollinaire's totally naïve
Rousseau.
If there is still room to entertain doubts about Henri Rousseau's
full understanding of his naïveté, if one could persuasively argue

that the painter was gradually educated to accept and cultivate his naïve style and to think of himself as a "modern primitive" who no longer needed to acquire the technical proficiency of the academic painters he admired, the same could never be said in the case of Lezama. Throughout his life Lezama was fully conscious of the implications of his poetics and of the need to cultivate his innocence and his naïveté in the face of the prevailing jaded attitude of modernism. Lezama is not a primitive but a wholehearted primitivist who is very conscious of the contributions of Henri Rousseau and Myshkin, as well as their reception by a world that seeks to equally praise and patronize them.

Lezama is attracted by the paintings and the person of Henri Rousseau and mentions them often in *Paradiso, Oppiano Licario,* and in his essays. Just as Cortázar has a reading of Lezama, he in turn has a very interesting reading of the person and works of Rousseau that can serve as a corrective to the portrait of Lezama as an ingenuous artist. Throughout his works Lezama employs Rousseau as an artistic alter ego, and through a process of identification similar to that experienced by Cortázar toward him, projects onto the French painter many concerns of his own. As in the case of Cortázar, many concerns are truly common to both artists though the final portrait that emerges is not devoid of a form of myth-making that reveals as much about Lezama's preoccupations as Cortázar's reveal of his.

In *Paradiso,* for example, Lezama offers a rather detailed commentary on Rousseau's *Walking in the Forest* in which he focuses on the enigmatic juxtaposition of a woman with a parasol dressed for a city walk and the desolate forest in which she has paused.[31]

> *En la antítesis de ese silencio que persigue, en otras ocasiones al despertar recordaba* La Promenade, *aquel extraño bosque donde el aduanero Rousseau pinta a su esposa extraviada en un silencio que no quiere quebrar, portando un paraguas para una lluvia imposible, amuleto que parece entregado por su esposo para evitar cualquier sorpresa en ese extraño paseo. A pesar de la natural sorpresa de la esposa por haberse extraviado en el bosque, parece sentirse acompañada. Aquí el silencio no persigue, acompaña. Es nada más que el primer espejo alucinante del bosque, al lado está el camino de regreso. El esposo pintor parece que ha querido colocar a su dama en esa delicadeza de un instante de miedo. Pero la esposa muestra una extrañeza reposada, pues sabe que en cualquier momento de peligro el pintor acudirá en su ayuda. Entonces, ella le entregará su paraguas. (*Obras completas, *1: 323–324)

· · ·

Henri Rousseau, *Walking in the Forest* (c. 1886). Oil on canvas, 27 9/16″ × 23 13/16″. Collection, Kunsthaus Zürich.

In the antithesis of the [stalking] silence, [on other occasions upon wak-
ing up he remembered] *La Promenade*, that strange forest where the
Douanier Rousseau paints his wife, lost in a silence that she tries not to
break, carrying an umbrella against an impossible rain, an amulet [that
seems given to her] by her husband to avert surprises on that strange
walk. The wife is naturally surprised at being lost in the woods, but still
she seems to feel accompanied. Here, the silence does not pursue, it
accompanies. It is nothing more than the first [hallucinating mirror] of
the woods, the path back is just over here. The painter husband seems
to have lured his lady in that delicacy of an instant of fear. The wife
shows a restful strangeness, knowing that in any moment of danger the
painter will come to her aid. Then she will hand him her umbrella.
(*Paradiso*, trans. Rabassa, pp. 229–230)

But it is in *Oppiano Licario* that Lezama presents a full-fledged interpretation of Rousseau's character and his works. Henri Rousseau
is discussed at length in the first chapter of the novel by several
characters. Whatever its contribution to the appreciation of the
French painter, Lezama's extensive discourse on Rousseau also serves
as the Cuban writer's poetic testament. The poetics that are ascribed
to Rousseau in *Oppiano Licario* are recognizably Lezama's own. The
stress of Lezama's commentary on the painter (the rejection of spiritual weariness and sadness and his manner of knowledge) parallels
Cortázar's own emphasis in "To Reach Lezama Lima."

Lezama devotes about eighteen pages of *Oppiano Licario* to the
discussion of "El Aduanero" (as he invariably calls him) and his
paintings. Whereas in *Paradiso* the commentary on Rousseau's
Walking in the Forest seems ultimately attributable to the thought
processes of José Cemí as reported by the domineering Lezaman narrator, in *Oppiano Licario* Lezama's views are dramatized principally
through three characters: the painter Luis Champollion, Fronesis,
and Cidi Galeb. A fourth character, Margaret McLearn, contributes
some comments about the emblematic aspect of painting before
yielding to a drunken stupor. This symposium takes place in Paris
at the painter's fourth-floor apartment in the Rue du Dragon. The
Rousseau episode of *Oppiano Licario* is treated in the special manner Lezama reserves for privileged passages in his work. Jewel-like,
it is carefully mounted on a setting designed to highlight its best
qualities. Lezama strategically positions the passage after Fronesis's
ambulatory meditation about emblems and signs.

Fronesis había encontrado un apartamento en el centro de la Isla de
Francia. Le gustaba, cuando salía de su casa, ir recorriendo las distin-

tas capas concéntricas del crecimiento de la ciudad. Mientras ca-
minaba a la caída de la tarde, volvía siempre a su recuerdo, la frase de
Gerardo de Nerval: el blasón es la clave de la historia de Francia. La
suma pizarrosa de los techos, los clavos en la puertas, el olor de un
asado desprendido por alguna ventana entreabierta, lo llevaban a
través de sus sentidos, a la comprobación de los fundamentos de la
frase de Nerval. Mientras atravesaba aquel laberinto, parecía que al
repetir mentalmente el blasón es . . . el blasón es . . . volviera a la luz
sucesiva. Calle tras calle iba comprobando cómo el blasón estaba en la
raíz de las órdenes de caballería, cómo de esas órdenes había surgido la
diversidad de los gremios. Cómo de esas corporaciones había nacido el
rico simbolismo del arte heráldico. De esos emblemas había cobrado
esplendor casi todo el arte medieval francés, estatuaria, sepulcros, tap-
icería, sillerías de coro. Pensaba después en Nicolás Flamel, en la calle
donde había vivido, calle de los Notarios, cerca de la Capilla de San-
tiago de la Boucherie, y cuyas mezclas de piedra roja y mercurio le
habían dado un oro para levantar hospitales y casas para pobres, al
mismo tiempo que con sus jeroglíficos en el cuarto arco del Cementerio
de los Inocentes, intentaba preparar las ánimas para la resurrección. Al
final de aquel laberinto, Fronesis tenía la seguridad de que no estaba
en el mundo minoano, de hilos sutiles y toros genitores, sino veía cómo
se alzaba de aquella casa el santo cáliz, la copa volante con una in-
scripción: multa signa facit. *El laberinto remontaba hasta el signo en*
aquella ciudad, cada calle ofrecía las metamorfosis del blasón. (p. 19)

. . .

Fronesis had found an apartment in the center of the Ile de France [Ile de
la Cité]. He liked, when he left his home, to gradually traverse the different concentric layers of the city's growth. While he walked at nightfall,
Gérard de Nerval's phrase: the coat of arms is the key to the history of
France, would always come to his mind. The slaty sum of the roofs,
the nails on the doors, the smell of a roast given off by a half-opened
window, would take him through his senses to the verification of the
grounds for Nerval's phrase. As he went through that labyrinth, it
seemed that by repeating "the coat of arms is . . . the coat of arms
is . . ." he would return to the successive light. Street after street he
would verify how the coat of arms was at the root of the orders of chivalry, how from these orders had emerged the diversity of the guilds.
How from these corporations the rich symbolism of heraldic art had
been born. From those emblems almost all of French medieval art had
gained splendor: statuary, tombs, tapestry, choir stalls. Later he thought
of Nicholas Flamel, of the street where he had lived, the street of the
Notaries, near the Chapel of Saint Jacques de la Boucherie, whose combinations of red stone and mercury had yielded a gold to raise hospitals

and poorhouses, while at the same time with his hieroglyphs in the fourth arch of the Cemetery of the Innocents he sought to prepare souls for resurrection. At the end of that labyrinth, Fronesis had the certainty that he was not in the Minoan world of subtle threads and engendering bulls, instead he saw how from that house the holy chalice rose, the flying goblet with an inscription: *multa signa facit*. The labyrinth went back to the sign in that city, each street offered the metamorphoses of the coat of arms.

Fronesis's meditation follows the evolution of emblems in French history from the heraldry of the age of chivalry and the guilds to the signs of alchemy and finally to the emblem of the Holy Grail and the legend *multa signa facit* ["he performs many signs"], whose proclamation of sign as miracle sets the proper tone for the discussion of Rousseau's poetics.

Fronesis wends his way through the streets of old Paris (a cityscape embroidered with medieval coats of arms) to the home of Champollion, whom he had met through Cemí in Havana. Lezama spares no opportunity for symbolism in this passage. The last name of the painter (a maker of emblems and signs) evokes one of history's most famous readers of emblems, Jean-François Champollion (1790–1832), the French archeologist who, thanks to the discovery of the Rosetta Stone, was the first to decipher Egyptian hieroglyphs. The painter's address "la Rue du Dragon" itself is emblematic, pointing to the medieval imagery that has been developed in the passage and at the same time to Lezama's own use of the dragon as an emblem for his poetic system.[32] The symbolism of the number four which appears both in the fourth-floor apartment and in the four persons present in the apartment is both a Judeo-Christian and a classical emblem for Lezama. In the Judeo-Christian tradition the number four alludes to the emblem of emblems, the Tetragrammaton, YHWH, the name of God, in Cabalistic practice the name whose pronunciation can unlock all hidden knowledge.[33] But the classical tradition of that numerical emblem is also operative in this passage. Throughout his writings Lezama refers to the classical bacchic concept of the fourth cup of wine (or any alcoholic drink) as "la cuarta copa, la copa de la demencia" ("the fourth cup, the cup of madness"). By the time Fronesis arrives at the fourth floor of the Street of the Dragon, both Champollion and his roommate Margaret McLearn (a didactic name if there ever was one) have reached at least that stage of bacchic possession. The ritual significance of the fourth cup is what she alludes to when she remarks to Champollion: "No merecía la pena tomarse cuatro cervezas, para seguir tu solfeo en la conversa-ción" (pp. 21–22) ("It's not worth the trouble of drinking four beers to follow your plodding conversation.")

Steeped in the meditation of emblems, Fronesis enters the bacchic studio of the painters and is invited by Champollion to display his knowledge of Henri Rousseau:

> *Champollion extrajo de un estante un cuaderno del Aduanero. Y prosi-*
> *guió, recuperando la alegría al señalarle el cuadro* El poeta y la musa:
> *idiomas, instrumentos musicales, viajes, lo que le habían enseñado y*
> *la pintura que a su vez enseñaba, amistades creadoras y conversables,*
> *en fin, todo lo que sabía se le había convertido en naturaleza alegre, en*
> *fiesta de la navidad con el gato sobre el tejado. Ni la tristeza, ni el*
> *cansancio del conocer aparecen nunca en su pintura ni en su persona,*
> *conoce la sombra del árbol de la vida. El cuenco de la mano y la copa*
> *le dan a beber la misma agua de vida, ¿qué crees tú, Fronesis, de esa*
> *manera de conocimiento del Aduanero?* (p. 31)

· · ·

> Champollion drew a notebook of the Douanier from a shelf. And he
> continued, recovering joy as he showed him the painting *The Poet and*
> *the Muse:* languages, musical instruments, voyages, what they had
> taught him and painting which in turn taught, creative and conversa-
> tional friendships, finally, all that he knew had become joyful nature for
> him, a Christmas party with the cat on the roof. Neither the sadness,
> nor the weariness of knowledge ever appear in his painting or in his
> person, he knows the shade of the tree of life. The hollow of his hand
> and the cup offer him the same water of life. Fronesis, what do you
> think of the Douanier's manner of knowledge?

Champollion is struck by the total absence of the weariness of knowledge in Rousseau's person and his paintings, the same trait that Cortázar admires in Lezama. From the beginning the question established for the symposium at the Rue du Dragon is an epistemo-logical one. In fact, the whole passage is itself an "epistemology" a discourse on knowledge. The issue is not so much the artist or his paintings but his manner of knowing, his mode of knowledge.

It is significant that Fronesis characterizes the ethics of Rousseau's painting in the same terms used to expound the ethics of Lezama in *Paradiso*.[34] There are two types of knowledge, one that leads to sal-vation and the other, founded in satanic pride, that leads to Hell.

> *El arte del Aduanero Rousseau—le respondió Fronesis—brota del sur-*
> *tidor inmóvil de un encantamiento. Su afición por la flauta parecía con-*

*vertirlo en el encantador de la familia, de las hojas, de la amistad, de
las casas de su pueblo, que al alejarlas parecen castillos de libros de
horas, de iglesias que al acercarlas a un primer plano quisieran dejarse
acariciar por la mano. Es el encantador del coyote mexicano y del león
de San Jerónimo. Sabe lo que tiene que saber, sabe lo necesario para su
salvación, no con el soplo de Marsyas o de Pan bicorne, cuya zampoña
lleva el aire agudizado hacia los infiernos descencionales, sino la flauta
de prolongaciones horizontales, del dios de la justicia alegre y de la
suprema justicia poética. (p. 31)*

• • •

The art of the Douanier Rousseau—answered Fronesis—springs from
the motionless fountain of an enchantment. His fondness for the flute
seemed to turn him into the charmer of the family, of leaves, of friendship, of the houses of his town which from afar look like castles in
books of hours, of churches which close up would like to let the hand
caress them. He is the charmer of the Mexican coyote and of Saint
Jerome's lion. He knows what he has to know, he knows what is necessary for his salvation, not with the breath of Marsyas or of two-horned
Pan, whose reed pipe takes the sharpened air to descending hells, but
with the flute of horizontal lengths of the god of joyful justice and of
supreme poetic justice.

Not accidentally, a similar image, in this case of the classical double
flute, is used by Cortázar in "The Idol of the Cyclades" to represent
life and discord, as Somoza explains to Morand: "The double flute,
like the one of the statuette that we saw in the museum in Athens.
The sound of life on the left, that of discord on the right" (p. 74).

In Fronesis's discourse Lezama focuses with consuming interest
on Rousseau's alleged ingenuousness, repeating the legendary anecdotes propagated by Apollinaire and Uhde:

*Este bretón vive un saludable hedonismo de burgués provinciano en el
barrio de Plaisance. Cuando se burlan de él, no hace esfuerzos por pa-
recer grave y agresivo, sino por el contrario, cree ver en esos guiños la
apreciación de su fuerza y el anticipo ingenuo de la corona y el panteón
de la inmortalidad, en los cuales cree, como también cree en los viajes,
el vino de la amistad, los recuerdos del colegio y la fiesta de bodas.
Tiene que soportar que aún después de muerto, Apollinaire, que ha
sido el que más lo ha querido, lo llame, cierto que con mucho cariño,
"Herodías sentimental," "anciano suntuoso y pueril que el amor arras-
tró hacia los confines del intelectualismo," "los ángeles le impidieron
penetrar en el hombre vivo cuyo aduanero hubiera llegado a ser," "an-*

ciano con grandes alas," "pobre ángel viejo." Frases de un joven es-
tallante como el Apollinaire de 1910, cuando se encuentra con un viejo
burlado burlón como el Aduanero, que antes que él se ha abrazado con
las cuatro o cinco cosas esenciales para un artista. Ha estado en México
en su adolescencia, no en el cansancio de la madurez rebuscadora, a
despecho de las burlas se ha impuesto con todo su instinto alegre y,
antes de morir, vuelve a sacar de su baúl su vieja flauta con la que ha
domesticado a coyotes y serpientes. (Oppiano Licario, p. 32)

• • •

This Breton lives the healthy hedonism of a provincial bourgeois in the
neighborhood of Plaisance. When they mock him, he makes no effort
to appear grave and aggressive, but on the contrary, he takes those winks
as a sign of appreciation of his strength and the naïve foreshadowing of
the crown and the pantheon of immortality, in which he believes, just as
he believes in voyages, in the wine of friendship, school memories and
wedding feasts. He has to endure that even after he is dead, Apollinaire,
who has loved him more than anyone, will call him, although with
great affection, "Sentimental Herodias," "sumptuous and puerile old
man whom love dragged to the limits of intellectualism," "the angels
kept him from penetrating into the living man whose customs officer he
would have become," "old man with large wings," "poor old angel."
Phrases of a bursting young man like the Apollinaire of 1910, when he
meets a mocked mocking old man like the Douanier, who before him
has already embraced the four or five essential things for an artist. He
has been in Mexico in his adolescence, not in the weariness of a pedantic maturity. Despite the mockery, he has prevailed with all his joyful
instinct, and before dying, he once more draws from his trunk his old
flute with which he has tamed coyotes and snakes.

Identifying with a Rousseau who is already dead by the time
Apollinaire pens his phrases of patronizing praise, Lezama bristles at
the young man's condescension, remarking that the old painter has,
long before the poet, embraced the essential aspects of art. Once
more Lezama's defense of Rousseau recalls Cortázar's defense of
Lezama in "To Reach Lezama Lima": ". . . when I was in Cuba I met
young intellectuals who smiled ironically remembering how Lezama
capriciously pronounced the name of some foreign poet. The difference began when those young people, called upon to say something about the poet in question, couldn't go beyond good phonetics
while Lezama in five minutes of speaking about the poet would
leave them staring at the ceiling" (p. 52). The Rousseau that emerges
from Lezama's pen is a mocked old man who himself is given to

mocking, but who is also capable of speaking of his own work with great pride:

> *Este viejo socarrón, que soporta las burlas de la vecinería, tiene también los supremos engallamientos. Así, un día se encuentra con Picasso y le dice: "Nosotros somos los dos grandes pintores vivientes, usted en la manera egipcia y yo en la manera moderna." (Oppiano Licario, p. 32)*
>
> · · ·
>
> This crafty old man, who puts up with the mockery of his neighbors, is also capable of supreme cockiness. Thus, one day, he runs into Picasso and says to him: "We are the two great living painters, you in the Egyptian manner and I in the modern manner."

This famous anecdote which has often been related to demonstrate Henri Rousseau's naïveté is reported by Lezama with an opposite motivation. Lezama perceives an insight in Rousseau's remark and seeks to understand it. His speculations about what Rousseau may have meant by Picasso's "Egyptian manner" are less valuable than his attempt to explain Rousseau's modernity.

> *El Aduanero, dentro de lo que él consideraba la tenacidad de su manera, presumía frente a Picasso de representar la manera moderna tal vez porque sus recuerdos de infancia le sirvieron para todo ulterior desenvolvimiento, por su fabuloso viaje a México, tan servicial a su imaginación como el de Baudelaire por las Indias americanas, por su alucinado culto del detalle y su místico y alegre sentido de la totalidad, por su originalidad en el sentido de poderosa raíz germinativa y no a través de síntesis de fragmentos aportados por las culturas. Su misticismo libre y su júbilo dentro de la buena canción. Con todas esas lecciones alegres y con todos esos laberintos resueltos, el Aduanero podía considerarse con justeza un excelente representante de la manera moderna, candorosa, alucinada, fuerte, frente a las potencias infernales.*
> (pp. 32–33)
>
> · · ·
>
> The Douanier, within what he considered the tenacity of his manner, presumed before Picasso to represent the modern manner perhaps because his childhood memories served him for all subsequent development, because of his fabulous trip to Mexico, as useful to his imagination as Baudelaire's through the American Indies, because of his hallucinated cult of detail and his mystical and joyful sense of totality, because of his originality in the sense of a powerful germinative root and not through a synthesis of fragments contributed by cultures. His

free mysticism and his jubilation within the good song. With all those happy lessons and all those solved labyrinths, the Douanier could justly consider himself an excellent representative of the modern manner, candid, hallucinated, strong, before the infernal powers.

It is evident that Lezama understands Rousseau and his "tenacious manner" very well, but it is equally evident that there is a high level of identification and "creative assimilation" in Lezama's definition of modernity. The Cuban writer, cognizant of the parallels between his poetics and those of the French painter, highlights their common ground. He stresses the crucial role of childhood memories in the work of Rousseau, so important in Lezama's own work. Rousseau's "adolescent" trip to Mexico[35] and the supposed exoticism that it planted in the painter's soul has its parallel in Lezama's own trip to Mexico in 1949 (one of the two he undertook as an adult, the other being to Jamaica in 1950).[36] It is not difficult to accept mysticism, joy, candor, hallucination, and opposition to the powers of Hell as shared elements in the poetics of Rousseau and Lezama; it is harder, however, to accept them as the norm for modernity!

Lezama's investigation of Rousseau's alleged primitivism (principally through Fronesis) summarizes the standard attitudes toward the painter's work but proposes a surprising third possibility that may be more convincing in the case of Lezama than in that of Rousseau.

En realidad . . . ¿fue Rousseau un pintor primitivo o un pintor popular, es decir, había en su arte un impedimento o una insuficiencia? ¿Tenía como los primitivos un mundo plástico que al intentar reproducirlo se quedaba en sus impedimentos? ¿Expresaba como el pueblo con lo que tenía y contaba, con recursos intuitivos, sin agazaparse el reto de las formas? O una ulterior posición ante sus obras, ¿había en él una malicia de los estilos detrás de sus órficos encantamientos? (p. 33)

• • •

In truth . . . was Rousseau a primitive painter or a painter of the people, that is to say, in his art was there an impediment or an insufficiency? Did he, like primitives, have a plastic world which when he attempted to reproduce it would stay in its impediments? Did he, like the people, express himself with what he had and could depend on, with intuitive means, without cowering from the challenge of forms? Or an ulterior position before his works: Was there a slyness of styles behind his Orphic enchantments?

Here Lezama reacts to the characterization of Henri Rousseau as a *naïf*. The introduction of the element of guile places the painter in command and frees him from the patronizing attitude of Apollinaire and company. It also permits Lezama to posit a reading of *The Muse Inspiring the Poet*, the portrait Rousseau did of Apollinaire and Marie Laurencin, that turns the tables by suggesting that the painter patronizes his patronizing patrons. Continuing his line of thought, Fronesis argues:

> *En esa expresión de lo popular, colocaría también* El poeta y su musa. *Es cierto que las medidas de las caras están tomadas a compás, pero parece que el Aduanero ha querido pintar un arquetipo burlón, visto por un provinciano que con todo el aluvión sanguíneo de su alegría, quiere dejar a sus amigos en una aceptación interrogante.* (p. 33)
>
> • • •
>
> In that expression of the popular, I would also place *The Poet and His Muse*. It is true that the faces have been traced with a compass, but it seems that the Douanier has wanted to paint a mocking archetype, seen by a provincial who with all of his sanguine torrent of joy wants to leave his friends in a questioning acceptance.

At this point in the reading, however, Lezama abandons the tentative tone, and the possibility of Rousseau's "malicia de los estilos" becomes a certainty:

> *Por candorosa que pueda haber sido la imaginación representativa del Aduanero, es indudable que al mostrar a Apollinaire con una pluma de ganso en una mano y un rollo de papeles en la otra, al mostrar a Marie Laurencin como un espectro ceñido de verticales listones lilas, señalando con el índice alzado la gloria del Empíreo, dejaba bien impresa la marca de que* era un amigo malicioso que quería satisfacer la ingenuidad que aquellos dos artistas esperaban de él. (p. 33; emphasis added)
>
> • • •
>
> Candid as the representative imagination of the Douanier may have been, it is undoubtable that in showing Apollinaire with a goose quill in one hand and a scroll of papers in the other, in showing Marie Laurencin as a specter girded by vertical lilac stripes, pointing with her raised index to the glory of the Empireum, he was leaving a clear enough mark that *he was a sly friend who wanted to satisfy the ingenuousness that those two artists expected of him.* (emphasis added)

Henri Rousseau, *The Muse Inspiring the Poet* (second version, 1909). Oil on canvas, 57 1/2″ × 38 1/2″. Öffentliche Kunstsammlung, Basel, Kunstmuseum.

In the subsequent discussion of other paintings (*Summer* in particular) Lezama seems to resurrect a "primitive phase" in Rousseau (p. 34), but in the case of the portrait of Apollinaire he adopts the position that the painter wanted to satisfy the expectations that the sitters for the portrait had of him. Doubtless this reading would have reassured Max Weber on the score of Rousseau's mastery of proportions, but it would have shattered his image of the old painter as a long-suffering martyr for art.[37]

Lezama vividly identifies with Rousseau's poetics, as he interprets them, and much of what he writes about the French painter is convincing and bespeaks a close kinship between certain aspects of their poetics. Their principal area of shared interest is the production of zones of enchantment. The following sensitive and intuitive characterization of Rousseau's art taken from *Oppiano Licario* is equally valid for Lezama. The peasants and horses of Rousseau's *Summer*

> *permanecen en su mundo interpretado.*[38] *Es el mundo del primitivo, no hay planos de superficie ni planos de profundidad, las cosas situadas en el lienzo tienen todas una importancia sagrada, son una caligrafía descifrada desde la pequeña hoja con sus líneas de secretos laberintos, hasta el sol que apoya la selva para su penetración. Una mano tiene un destino, una hoja tiene un secreto, un árbol su ámbito. El Aduanero estudia, distribuye, reordena una mano, una hoja, un árbol y en pago de esa humildad, se le hechiza un destino, un secreto, un ámbito.*
> (p. 35)
>
> . . .
>
> remain in their interpreted world. It is the world of the primitive, there are neither surface planes nor background planes, the things located on the canvas all have a sacred importance, they are a deciphered calligraphy from the small leaf with its lines of secret labyrinths to the sun that the jungle supports for its penetration. A hand has a destiny, a leaf has a secret, a tree its perimeter. The Douanier studies, distributes, reorders a hand, a leaf, a tree and in payment for that humility a destiny, a secret, a perimeter become enchanted.

Lezama perceives that for Rousseau as for himself art does not consist in depicting nature and life according to the conventions of realism. In their work there is no contrast between foreground and background; there is no perspective. Lezama's writing like Rousseau's painting is a sacred calligraphy that studies, distributes, and reorganizes the world in order to delimit a zone of enchantment.

Henri Rousseau, *The Sleeping Gypsy* (1897). Oil on canvas, 51″ × 6′7″. Collection, The Museum of Modern Art, New York. Gift of Mrs. Simon Guggenheim.

Perhaps one of the best examples of that zone of enchantment is Rousseau's *The Sleeping Gypsy,* and an excellent description of its enigma[39] is that given in *Oppiano Licario* by Cidi Galeb:

Sabemos que tiene que existir una extraña relación entre dos incom-prensibles cercanías, pero sabemos también que es inagotable su indes-cifrable liaison. . . . En el desierto, uno al lado del otro, el león y la gitana. El león, rastreando, la gitana durmiendo. Al lado de la gitana y de su sueño, el bastón, la mandolina y el porrón de agua. El león aun-que está a su lado, no parece tener ningún interés en acercársele, olfa-tea como con cierta sospecha. La gitana está escondida en su sueño, parece que mientras no despierte no tendrá que temer nada del león. Lo que menos enlaza a la gitana durmiente con la cercanía del león es la inminencia mortal. El hecho es que uno está al lado de la otra, lo in-descifrable es la lejanía de la muerte. Lo único que los une es parado-jalmente la diversidad de esos dos mundos, rastrear y dormir. Él busca un punto, se obstina en perseguirlo, no es la mujer dormida, pues está a su lado y él continúa rastreando. Nadie puede decir lo que busca y lo

*que desdeña. La inmensa defensa del sueño, en la mujer extendida en
el desierto, es su protección. . . . La pureza de El Aduanero está en
haber acercado la gitana al león, sin que quepa la menor posibilidad de
que sea destruida en el sueño. Su hechizo en esa situación es superior a
la distancia, a la causalidad y al hábito esperado. Es una eternidad
inocente y alegre, el león seguirá rastreando y la gitana durmiendo.*
(p. 38)

• • •

We know that a strange relationship has to exist between two incomprehensible proximities, but we also know that their indecipherable
liaison is inexhaustible. . . . In the desert, one beside the other, the lion
and the gypsy. The lion tracking, the gypsy sleeping. Beside the gypsy
and her sleep, the staff, the mandolin and the water jug. Even though the
lion is beside her he does not seem in the least interested in drawing
near, he sniffs as if with some suspicion. The gypsy is hidden in her
sleep, it seems that as long as she does not awake she won't have anything to fear from the lion. What least ties the sleeping gypsy to the
proximity of the lion is a mortal imminence. The fact is that one is
beside the other, what is indecipherable is the remoteness of death. The
only thing that joins them is paradoxically the diversity of those two
worlds, tracking and sleeping. He seeks a point, stubbornly pursues it, it
is not the sleeping woman since she is beside him and he continues
tracking. No one can say what he seeks and what he disdains. The immense defense of sleep, in the woman stretched out in the desert, is her
protection. . . . The purity of the Douanier lies in his having placed the
gypsy next to the lion without in the least allowing for the possibility of
her being destroyed in her sleep. His enchantment in that situation surpasses distance, causality and expectations. It is an innocent and happy
eternity, the lion will continue tracking and the gypsy sleeping.

In Rousseau's painting, Lezama recognizes his own trademark: the
triumph of juxtaposition over causality, the victory of the unexpected over convention.

I believe that Lezama's overinterpretation of *The Muse Inspiring
the Poet* is due to his strong identification with Rousseau. The ridicule of inflexible viewers and reviewers, or even the patronizing adop-
tion of Rousseau by avant-garde artists, critics, and dealers touches
a raw nerve in Lezama. Because of his close identification with
Rousseau, the Cuban writer sees the reception of Rousseau and his
paintings in terms of his own reception. The Dantesque punishment
that Lezama reserved for those who laughed at Rousseau's paintings
is probably the same that he felt his own detractors deserved:

Los miserables que se reían de él en presencia de ese cuadro ya maestro
[A Carnival Evening*], y de los dieciséis años que mandó al Salón de los*
Independientes obras ejemplares, estarán por siempre en las cazuelas
del infierno, rodeados de carcajadas y entre carcajadas estarán en el
desfile secular. Pues si alguna gloria fue evidente, serena, incontras-
table, alegre, fue la del Aduanero. (p. 41)

• • •

The wretches who laughed at him in the presence of that painting [*A*
Carnival Evening] which was already a masterpiece, and of the sixteen
years that he sent exemplary works to the Salon des Indépendants will
forever lie in the pots of Hell ringed by sneering laughter and amid
sneering laughter they will remain as the centuries pass. For if any glory
was evident, serene, invincible, happy, it was that of the Douanier.

The discourse on Henri Rousseau in *Oppiano Licario*, Lezama's
last and unfinished work, is both one more attempt on the part
of the Cuban writer at explaining his "poetic system" (this time
through the work of an artist with whom he deeply identifies) and
an opportunity to correct the reception of his own works and his person. In this his last bow Lezama tells those who would patronize
him and label him a primitive that he was a sly friend who did not
want to disappoint their expectations of his naïveté.

As his deep interest in "the case of Henri Rousseau" and in
Dostoevsky's Prince Myshkin amply reveal, Lezama's "naïveté" is
consciously cultivated. His ingenuousness is neither a social nor a
mental insufficiency but a rigorous artistic discipline that he mili-
tantly adopts. A letter that Lezama wrote to his nephew Orlando on
December 31, 1966, demonstrates the importance he accorded to
the cultivation of innocence in life and art. It is innocence that allows access to the epiphany, that central desideratum of art and life
for Lezama. Writing on the occasion of the upcoming feast of the
Epiphany, Lezama links the visit of the Magi to other epiphanies
in life:

Ahora ya está cerca la visita de los Reyes. Mientras el niño conserva su
estado de inocencia lo visitan los Reyes. Al paso del tiempo, mientras
su alma se encuentre en ese estado de inocencia, lo visitarán los pro-
digios, las sorpresas y le acudirán de nuevo los Reyes. Ese convenci-
miento de que algo va a suceder, de que lo excepcional y extraordinario
tocará a la puerta, llena de vida, de magia y de poesía. (p. 206)

• • •

> Now the visit of the Magi is already near. As long as a child preserves
> his state of innocence the Magi visit him. As time passes, while his soul
> is in that state of innocence, he will be visited by wonders, by surprises,
> and the Magi will once again come to him. That conviction that some-
> thing is going to happen, that the exceptional and the extraordinary will
> knock at the door fills one with life, with magic, and with poetry.

Rousseau has also left sufficient proof of his conscious preservation
of his innocence and a clear awareness of the tenacity of his manner
in the letter quoted above where he explains to a critic that he has
kept his naïveté on the advice of the Academic painters Gérôme and
Clément and confidently asserts that he cannot change the manner
that he has "acquired by stubborn application."

The similarities between Lezama and Rousseau extend far beyond
the pattern of the reception of their works. They share a belief in the
conscious cultivation of their childlike nature and the need to apply
themselves stubbornly to their naïve manner. Their cultivation of
innocence, in turn, is directly related to the central concern of their
poetics. Implicitly in the case of Rousseau and explicitly in that of
Lezama, the main concern of their art is the creation of zones of enchantment. They create these zones by means of paradoxical juxtapositions that elicit a rich sense of enigma in their viewers or readers. The ultimate goal for both is epiphany. In Lezama's case it is an
extensively articulated theory with ethical as well as aesthetic di-
mensions, but, as at least one critic has noted, "spatial epiphanies"
are also at the heart of Rousseau's art.[40] Likewise both painter and
writer seek to banish time from their works and thereby induce an
impression of timelessness and stasis. The importance of "la fijeza"
for Lezama's poetics is well known; it is equally important in the
work of Rousseau: "Rousseau's and Seurat's depictions of working-
class holiday life share a sense of quietude and stasis that imparts
the fixity of eternal order to the banal subject matter."[41] Shattuck
attributes this timelessness to Rousseau's special handling of light.[42]

Ultimately the major and most evident similarity of Rousseau's
and Lezama's art is that their technique is superficial, that is, in-
tensely concerned with the surface. This too is a consequence of
their cultivation of a childlike vision. Since the concepts of perspective, priority, and hierarchy are totally absent from their work, there
is no play between foreground and background—all is foregrounded.
This has led both Shattuck and Cortázar to speak of the technique of
Rousseau and Lezama respectively in terms of jewelry. Shattuck
feels that the cohesive force of Rousseau's painting is like that of

Henri Rousseau, *A Carnival Evening* (1886). Oil on canvas, 46″ × 35 1/4″.
Philadelphia Museum of Art: Louis E. Stern Collection.

cloisonné: "No representation of three-dimensional space according to Renaissance tradition holds Rousseau's work together. It coheres according to a large-scale surface arrangement, similar to cloisonné. . . . Surface tension carries the unity of his compositions to the edges of the canvas" (*The Banquet Years*, p. 104). Cortázar, in turn, characterizes the reading of *Paradiso* as the successive examination of many pectorals: "the permanent fascination of a word by word reading, which at heart is the way to read that sorcerer's manual of wonders where each fragment is like a constellation, a pectoral, an incantation."[43]

Finally it is possible to return to the key question posed at the beginning of this chapter, and apply it to both artists: Are their original styles truly intentional or are they merely a consequence of defective technique? For Rousseau this question has already been answered for quite some time. The comparative study of his oil sketches for landscapes and the completed paintings reveals both a mastery of impressionist technique and the artist's clear intention to transform rather than copy reality. The conclusion reached by Carolyn Lanchner, one of the contributors to the catalog for the Museum of Modern Art's 1985 Rousseau exhibition, is that he painted the way he did because he wanted to rather than because he could not paint in any other way.[44]

It should also be clear by now that Lezama's style, far from being the result of defective technique, constitutes a bold attempt to redefine modernity. It is not surprising that Saúl Yurkievich, who has written with so much insight about Cortázar, should contribute a clear historical perspective on Lezama's modernity:

> Historically, Lezama Lima turns out to be a straggling symbolist. As a member of a post-avant-garde group, he knows the aesthetic manifestations of his time, but he does not mentally set roots in the contemporary. . . . His poetics are regressive, they establish no connection with the technological revolution, they are alien to the notion of crisis, of collapse, of epistemic rupture. His innocent writing, his beatific vision, remain immune to the disintegrating optic of the avant-garde, to any ontological lack. In Lezama Lima there are neither glimpses of a split consciousness nor of a faustic consciousness.[45]

Lezama's consciously innocent writing and his "beatific vision" require heroes different than those of his contemporary writers. If the model artist of Lezama's modernity is Henri Rousseau, then the model protagonist is Prince Myshkin. Undoubtedly, Cortázar was

aware of the six sonnets Lezama wrote in honor of Dostoevsky's protagonist when he spoke of the Myshkin side of Lezama. Each of the
sonnets carries an epigraph taken from *The Idiot*. The beautiful Sonnet VI praises Prince Myshkin's "wise foolishness" and vindicates
the poetics of innocence of Henri Rousseau and José Lezama Lima,
by asserting the transformational power of faith:

VI

*(¿Llevas contigo la cruz
que le compraste al soldado?)*

*Trae acá el dado con el que fuiste engañado,
si es de hojalata le rindo mis diamantes.
La cruz reemplazando el dado del soldado borrachito,
y Rajogine que quiere comprar en oro el engaño.*

*Viene bien que al comprar la cruz seamos engañados.
Es de oro, de oro, y la pagamos con doble pecho mío.
La pagamos con oro pirulero y es de lata
y contribuimos a que el soldado doble mejor la esquina.*

*Pero ahora, sutil, inconfesable, viene el otro pícaro barbado.
Sabe que la cruz pagada como oro, si es de lata,
es otra joya que rompe en la suprema esencia.*

*Y si al soldado se la adquirimos como oro al irse por la esquina,
el que llega sabiendo el pecho que la respira como lata,
quiere imantar con oro el nacimiento del fulgor en el engaño.* (Obras
completas, I: 837–838)

. . .

VI

(Are you carrying the cross
that you bought from the soldier?)

Bring here the die with which you were deceived,
if it is made of tin I yield it my diamonds.
The cross replacing the drunken soldier's die,
and Rogozhin who wants to buy the deceit with gold.

It is fitting to be deceived when we buy the cross.
It's of gold, of gold, and we paid for it with my double breast.
We paid for it with Peruvian gold and it's of tin
and we contributed to the soldier's better turning of the corner.

But now, subtle, unspeakable, comes the other bearded rogue.
He knows that a cross paid for as gold, if it's tin,
is another jewel that breaks into the supreme essence.

And if we acquired it from the soldier taking it for gold as he turned the
   corner,
the one who arrives knowing the breast that breathes it as tin,
wants to magnetize with gold the birth of splendor in deceit.

Like this sonnet, all of Lezama's work is founded on alchemy, but it
is not the alchemy of Mallarmé or Borges; it is an alchemy seldom
found among the moderns, the alchemy of faith.

Notes

1. Introduction: Beyond the Aesthetics of Realism

1. If we can abstract the fundamental elements of any narrative, they might be characterized as *description* and *narration*. In this broad sense, description fills the space of the novel with objects, images, and settings while narration advances the action and develops the plot. Gérard Genette makes this fruitful distinction between the descriptive and the narrative elements. I have more to say about its importance to Lezama's style in Chapter 2.

2. J. M. Alonso, "A Sentimental Realism," *Review* 12 (Fall 1974): 46.

3. Julio Rodríguez-Luis, *La literatura hispanoamericana entre compromiso y experimento*, p. 104.

4. See Rodríguez-Luis's characterization of Lezama's cultural underdevelopment, ibid., p. 108.

5. Emir Rodríguez Monegal, "*Paradiso:* Una silogística del sobresalto," *Revista Iberoamericana* 41, nos. 92–93 (1975): 527.

6. Mikhail Bakhtin, *Problems of Dostoevsky's Poetics*, ed. and trans. Caryl Emerson, p. 8.

7. The fact that Lezama shares Goethe's basic artistic viewpoint will not surprise readers. Lezama constantly invokes Goethe in his essays. It is also well known that *Wilhelm Meister* was a conscious model in Lezama's mind for *Paradiso*, and that the author referred to José Cemí as "un Wilhelm Meister habanero" ["A Havana Wilhelm Meister"]. Chapter 3 deals with the special importance of Goethe's *Bildungsroman* for Cemí.

8. Bakhtin, *Problems*, p. 27.

9. Among the *spoudogeloios* genres Bakhtin includes the mimes of Sophron, the Socratic dialogue, the literature of the Symposiasts, the early memoir literature of Ion of Chios and Critias, pamphlets, bucolic poetry, and Menippean satire (ibid., pp. 106–107).

10. Severo Sarduy, *Escrito sobre un cuerpo*, p. 89.

11. Sarduy's dialogue with Lezama can also be self-effacing and filial: "My work, in quotation marks, is therefore inserted let's say in the inaugural address of the teacher; I will not persist, of course, in public memory (despite the encyclopedia that already includes me), as a writer, nevertheless, I believe, and of this I *am* proud, and underscore my situation with great braggadocio, I believe that I will endure as the one who has seen, the one who has seen the teacher, the one who was able to point him out, I am not the first, of course, Cintio [Vitier] or José Rodríguez Feo saw him before me. But I am the first one who has realized his immensity and the one who, in

order to repeat a small text that I wrote in his homage, the one who knows that he lives in the Lezama Era" (Harold Alvarado Tenorio, "Con Severo Sarduy en el Café de Flore," *El Mundo* [Medellín], November 24, 1979, p. 15, quoted in Roberto González Echevarría, *La ruta de Severo Sarduy*, p. 56).

12. Enrico Mario Santí, "Párridiso," *Modern Language Notes* 94 (1979): 360. Also in *José Lezama Lima: Textos críticos*, ed. Justo Ulloa, pp. 116–117.

13. For a discussion of Sarduy's basic strategies of derision, see Gustavo Pellón, "Severo Sarduy's Strategy of Irony: Paradigmatic Indecision in *Cobra* and *Maitreya*," *Latin American Literary Review* 12, no. 23 (1983): 7–13.

14. Severo Sarduy, *Maitreya*, p. 187.

15. Roberto González Echevarría, "Memoria de apariencias y ensayo de *Cobra*," in *Relecturas: Estudios de literatura cubana*, p. 143. For the best-informed discussion of Sarduy's works, see González Echevarría's *La ruta de Severo Sarduy*.

2. The Aesthetics of Excess: The Novel as Fibroma

1. For a lucid evaluation of Lezama's modernity see Rubén Ríos-Avila, "The Origin and the Island: Lezama and Mallarmé," *Latin American Literary Review* 8, no. 16 (1980): 242–255. Ríos-Avila argues convincingly that the difference between Mallarmé and Lezama lies in their attitude toward the act of poetic creation. For Mallarmé it is tragic: "The poet, unlike God, is consumed and invalidated by his own creation" (p. 251), while for Lezama it is celebratory: "The poetic act, therefore, is not the suppression of respiration, but a 'Science of breathing.' The I is adequated to the universal respiratory rhythm of being: the search for a pure objective rhythm. A poem formalizes and transcends the rhythm of desire: it refamiliarizes man with his purified Form" (p. 251).

2. Roberto González Echevarría, "Apetitos de Góngora y Lezama," in *Relecturas: Estudios de literatura cubana*, p. 113.

3. "Zen Buddhism," *Encyclopedia of Philosophy*, 1967 ed., 8: 367. Severo Sarduy pays equivocal homage to his "Zen master," Lezama, by parodying the practice of Zen paradoxes in *Maitreya*. In that novel we are told that a Tibetan lama "Respondía a todo koen con un eructo, una trompetilla, o el fácil aforismo 'samsara es nirvana'" (p. 54). ("He answered every koan with a burp, a Bronx cheer, or the facile aphorism 'Samsara is Nirvana.'")

4. In "Apetitos de Góngora y Lezama," González Echevarría, glossing a passage of Lezama's essay "Sierpe de don Luis de Góngora" ("Don Luis de Góngora's Serpent"), discusses the contrast (and the complementarity) Lezama sees between Góngora and St. John of the Cross: "The movement toward plenitude leads either to repetition and the accumulation of figures, metaphors—to nonsense, to madness—, or by the correlative and opposite path to the void, to the unanimous night which erases every trace. If on the one hand we have satiety, a plenitude never reached, on the other we find the negation of all appetite . . . The smoothness of St. John's poetry, the absence of adjectives, the reduction of language to verbs and nouns, and sometimes only to interjections, is the other face of baroque heterogeneity; . . .

two moments of the same movement toward the recuperation of the poetic voice—negative in St. John, assimilative in the baroque. The white page, the black page, saturated with signs: a counterpoint of silences" (*Relecturas*, pp. 108–109). Besides this stylistic complementarity, González Echevarría also suggests that for Lezama St. John's faith fills the void of Góngora's alleged nihilism.

    5. Oppiano Licario's "koan" reads as follows:

José Cemí

No lo llamo, porque él viene,
como dos astros cruzados
en sus leyes encaramados
la órbita elíptica tiene.

Yo estuve, pero él estará,
cuando yo sea el puro conocimiento,
la piedra traída en el viento,
en el egipcio paño de lino me envolverá.

La razón y la memoria al azar
verán a la paloma alcanzar
la fe en la sobrenaturaleza.

La araña y la imagen por el cuerpo,
no puede ser, no estoy muerto.
Vi morir a tu padre; ahora, Cemí, tropieza.
(José Lezama Lima, *Obras completas* 1:644)
. . .

José Cemí

I don't call him, because he comes,
like two stars that cross
in their exalted laws,
he knows their elliptical orbit.

I was, but he will be,
when I am pure knowledge,
the stone brought on the wind,
he will wrap me in Egyptian linen.

Reason and memory by chance
will see the dove attain
faith in the super-natural.

The spider and the image in place of body
cannot be, I am not dead.
I saw your father die; and now, Cemí, stumble.
(*Paradiso*, trans. Gregory Rabassa, p. 465)

    6. Lezama usually omits the accent in the word *sólo*. I respect his orthography throughout. For a discussion of Lezama's orthography, mispellings, and errors, see Julio Cortázar, "Para llegar a Lezama Lima," in *La vuelta al*

día en ochenta mundos, 2:41–81. For Sarduy's attitude see "Dispersión: Falsas notas/homenaje a Lezama" in *Escrito sobre un cuerpo,* p. 63. Enrico Mario Santí's "Párridiso," which takes into account Cortázar's and Sarduy's comments, is the most complete and thought-provoking study of this aspect of Lezama's writing.

7. Emir Rodríguez Monegal, "*Paradiso:* Una silogística del sobresalto," p. 523.

8. About the fibroma Julio Ortega writes, "it is not accidental that even the fibroma extracted from the mother is contemplated in the novel as a necessary and dazzling object" ("La biblioteca de José Cemí," *Revista Iberoamericana* 41, nos. 92–93 [1975]: 519). In *Paradiso y el sistema poético de Lezama Lima,* Margarita Junco Fazzolari sees an analogy between the fibroma and poetry: "It is possible to isolate poetry and capture it in the poem, in the same manner that in this passage the fibroma has been separated to preserve it in a glass jar" (p. 92).

9. For a list of José Cemí's epiphanies see Rodríguez Monegal, "*Paradiso:* Una silogística del sobresalto," pp. 530–531. His list does not include the episode of the fibroma.

10. For a thorough discussion of paradigmatic and syntagmatic relations, see "Syntagma and Paradigm" in Oswald Ducrot and Tzvetan Todorov, *Encyclopedic Dictionary of the Sciences of Language,* trans. Catherine Porter, pp. 106–111. See also John Lyons, *Introduction to Theoretical Linguistics,* pp. 70–76.

11. For the role of asthma in *Paradiso,* see Ortega, "La biblioteca de José Cemí," p. 511. See also Fazzolari, *Paradiso y el sistema poético,* p. 60.

12. Lezama shares the Baroque fascination with monsters and monstrosity. For a study of the image of the monster in a writer of the Spanish Golden Age, see Roberto González Echevarría, "El 'Monstruo de una especie y otra': *La vida es sueño,* 3, 2, p. 725," in *Calderón: Códigos, Monstruo, Icones,* ed. Javier Herrero, pp. 27–58.

13. Lezama's idiosyncratic use of the *ouroboros* requires clarification. Usual interpretations of the *ouroboros* dwell on the cycle of destruction and renewal. For the purposes of his symbolism (here and in other passages), Lezama focuses on the aspect of self-destruction. As shown in Chapter 3, circularity has specially negative connotations in Lezama's imagery.

González Echevarría has used the image of the *ouroboros* to describe the "incompleteness" Lezama sees in Góngora: "The madness, the 'incompleteness' of Góngora lies in the fact that appetite must always be infinite and circular—the snake that devours itself and makes itself disappear, that coils and annuls itself" (*Relecturas,* p. 111).

14. The concept of "not rejecting" recurs in Lezama's writing. See, for example, his essays from *Tratados en La Habana,* "El *no rechazar* teresiano" (*Obras completas,* 2:495–499), "Veces que el americano no rechazó," (2:499–503).

15. Gérard Genette, *Figures II,* p. 58.

16. Zosimos (fl. 300 A.D.), a contemporary of Tertullian and Saint Clement of Alexandria, was the author of the *Cheirokmeta,* one of the earliest

Attempt3

works on alchemy in Greek. He left accounts of alchemical visions in which he experienced gnosis. See Allison Coudert, *Alchemy: The Philosopher's Stone.* See also "Alchemy," *Dictionary of the History of Ideas* (1973).

3. The Ethics of Androgyny: A Sexual Parable

1. For the concept of *dépense,* see Georges Bataille, "La Notion de dépense," in *Oeuvres complètes,* 1:302–320. See also Severo Sarduy, "Del Yin al Yang (Sobre Sade, Bataille, Marmori, Cortázar y Elizondo," in *Escrito sobre un cuerpo,* pp. 9–30.

2. For these polemics see Emir Rodríguez Monegal, *Narradores de esta América,* vol. 2, pp. 133–135. See also the discussion of this issue in the open letters by Vargas Llosa and Rodríguez Monegal, pp. 141–155.

3. Enrique Lihn, "*Paradiso,* novela y homosexualidad," *Hispamérica* 8, no. 22 (1979): 14. For a more positive view of Foción, see Raymond D. Souza, *Major Cuban Novelists,* p. 63. For a clear exposition of characterization in *Paradiso,* see "The Paradigm of Characterization," Chapter 3 of Souza's *The Poetic Fiction of José Lezama Lima,* pp. 38–52.

4. Lihn, "*Paradiso,* novela y homosexualidad," pp. 16–17.

5. For a different view, see Gustavo Pérez Firmat, "Descent into *Paradiso:* A Study of Heaven and Homosexuality," *Hispania* 59, no. 2 (1976): 247–257, where he makes a case for Cemí's homosexuality and argues that "throughout the novel homosexuality and androgyny are identified" (p. 254). Pérez Firmat also gives a very useful explanation of the Taoist symbolism in *Paradiso* (p. 255).

6. Regarding the characters of *Paradiso,* Lezama has remarked: "I found that poetry bubbled, boiled, as if yearning to become another world; each metaphor was becoming a character, each image was becoming a situation in the novel and then, somewhat magically, as in the carpet of Baghdad, I was transported from poetry to the novel" (Centro de Investigaciones Literarias de la Casa de las Américas, *Interrogando a Lezama Lima,* p. 29).

For the characters as parts of one personality see Fazzolari, *Paradiso y el sistema poético:* "The three are part of the same personality, the divisions brought on by the Fall. They are the three parts of the soul according to German mystics: the instincts, reason, and the divine spark" (pp. 75–76). See also Lihn, "*Paradiso,* novela y homosexualidad," p. 6.

7. For a discussion of the concept of *phronesis* in Stoic philosophy, see Eleuterio Elorduy, S. J., *El estoicismo,* 2:146, 410; Emile Brehier, *Chrysippe et l'ancien Stoïcisme,* p. 236; and Edward V. Arnold, *Roman Stoicism,* p. 306.

8. González Echevarría has underscored the importance of the concept of *hypertelia:* "Lezama aspires in his work to the miracle, to the incarnation of the word. . . . That resurrection does not only reflect Lezama's evident Catholicism, but also represents the most radical aspect of his aesthetics. The resurrection is the world of poetry 'become substance,' of the hypertelia (beyond the end) to which many of his characters refer in several discussions, the superfluity to which we have alluded" ("Apetitos de Góngora y

Lezama," in *Relecturas*, p. 113). González Echevarría stresses here the significance of hypertelia in Lezama's aesthetic system. In this chapter I am primarily interested in the ethical dimension of hypertelia in *Paradiso* where both Foción and Cemí propose rival definitions of the concept.

9. D. B. Monro, *The Modes of Ancient Greek Music* (Oxford University Press, 1894), p. 64, quoted in Mercedes Cortázar, "Entering Paradise," *Review* 12 (Fall 1974): 19n.1.

10. Dante Alighieri, *The Divine Comedy: I, Inferno*, trans. John D. Sinclair, p. 189.

11. See André Gide, *Corydon*, in *Oeuvres complètes*, 9:226–227.

12. Souza interprets the passage as follows: "The tree is a dual image. On the one hand it represents Foción's obsession with Fronesis, and, on the other, it could represent the tree of life that embodies all the positive and negative aspects of existence. Foción's incessant circling of the tree reveals his attempts to control the chaos of his life and . . . to resolve the enigma of existence . . . The bolt of lightning that releases Foción indicates the sudden gaining of an illumination and insight that frees him from his obsessive anguish" (*Major Cuban Novelists*, p. 64). The only objection I find to Souza's interpretation concerns the lightning. If it signifies illumination, it is Cemí who benefits truly, and Foción's enlightenment would seem to be merely transitory.

13. Carmen Ruiz Barrionuevo, *El "Paradiso" de Lezama Lima*, p. 66, rightly sees this story which closes "Chapter 8's opening to Eros" as a warning to Cemí spoken by the voice of wisdom, Fronesis.

14. For a complete discussion of the history of the irregularities that bar men from the priesthood see "Irrégularités," *Dictionnaire de Théologie Catholique*. The major scriptural source cited by popes and councils of the Church is Leviticus 21:16–20: "None of your descendants, in any generation, must come forward to offer the food of his God if he has any infirmity—no man must come near if he has an infirmity such as blindness or lameness, if he is disfigured or deformed, if he has an injured foot or arm, if he is a hunchback or a dwarf, if he has a disease of the eyes or of the skin, if he has a running sore, or if he is a eunuch" (*Jerusalem Bible*). Another source is Deuteronomy 23:2. According to *The New Bible Commentary Revised*, ed. Donald Guthrie et al., p. 223, "The exclusion of emasculated persons was a protest against heathen cultic practices." In the early Church, the exclusion from the priesthood of eunuchs (particularly voluntary ones) was also an attempt to discourage imitation of the Church Father Origen, who castrated himself in order to escape temptation. The ghost of that heterodox Church Father, whose name in Spanish furnished the double meaning (origin/Origen) of Lezama's famous journal, *Orígenes*, seems to haunt these pages of *Paradiso*.

15. Coudert, *Alchemy*, p. 144.

16. Ibid., p. 142.

17. Ibid., p. 145.

18. Ibid.

19. *Aeschylus 1: Oresteia*, trans. Richmond Lattimore, pp. 112–113.

20. For a discussion of this doctrine, see Arnold, *Roman Stoicism*, pp. 190–192.

21. Eloísa Lezama Lima, in her edition of *Paradiso*, p. 477n.21, defines *dromomanía* as, "the mania which consists in moving incessantly from one place to another, or an exaggerated need to travel."

22. Fazzolari has already identified the undershirt with the *ouroboros* (*Paradiso y el sistema poético*, p. 90). Souza, instead, has discussed the passage in terms of geometric symbolism as a movement from "inner confusion to inner unity . . . The sexual act becomes then one of many manifestations of the search for meaning in life and the control over chaos" (*Major Cuban Novelists*, pp. 61–62).

23. The passage reads: "Quizá la resurrección de los cuerpos sea el verdadero nombre de lo que Fronesis [*sic*] llamó la hipertelia de la inmortalidad" (1 : 378) ("Perhaps the resurrection of [the] bodies is the [real] name of what Fronesis [*sic*] called the [hypertelia] of immortality" [p. 269]). Fazzolari (*Paradiso y el sistema poético*, p. 87) correctly ascribes the term and its homosexual definition to Foción. She sees in Foción's defense of homosexuality "the desire to prolong, through a false innocence, an immortality that was irremediably lost with the Fall of Man" (p. 86). In Foción's concept of homosexuality as a lost innocence I see a restatement of Corydon's argument: "Tout comme je crois, excusez mon audace, l'homosexualité dans l'un et l'autre sexe, plus spontanée, plus naïve que l'hétérosexualité" (*Gide, Corydon*, p. 280) ("Just as I believe, excuse my boldness, that homosexuality in either sex is more spontaneous, more naïve than heterosexuality").

24. I stress *Paradiso* because *Oppiano Licario*, Lezama's posthumous, unfinished novel, presents a more active José Cemí.

4. Culture as Nature: An American Practice of Reading and Writing

1. See Fazzolari, *Paradiso y el sistema poético*, and Eloísa Lezama Lima's introduction to her edition of *Paradiso*, especially pp. 31–46.

2. Cortázar, "Para llegar a Lezama Lima," pp. 57–58.

3. For a theoretical critique of "lo real maravilloso americano," see Roberto González Echevarría, *Alejo Carpentier: The Pilgrim at Home*, pp. 107–129. González Echevarría demonstrates Carpentier's essential contradiction: his definition of Americanness as an unproblematic acceptance of magic can only be reached via a skeptical European viewpoint that bespeaks the author's alienation from his culture.

4. The term "literature of exhaustion" was coined by John Barth in an essay about Borges: "The Literature of Exhaustion," *Atlantic Monthly* 220 (August 1967):29–34; also in Barth's *The Friday Book: Essays and Other Nonfiction*, pp. 62–76.

5. Enrico Mario Santí's penetrating article, "Lezama, Vitier y la crítica de la razón reminiscente" (*Revista Iberoamericana* 41, nos. 92–93 [1975]: 542–544), discusses this passage and explains Lezama's appropriation of Curtius' (and, as Santí discovers, Toynbee's) concept of history as fiction.

6. Centro de Investigaciones Literarias, *Interrogando*, p. 52.

7. T. S. Eliot, *Selected Essays*, p. 6.

8. The phrase "ear of the heart" and its variants recur in the writings of St. Augustine. See *The Confessions of St. Augustine*, trans. Rex Warner, 4, 5: "May I learn from you, who are Truth, and may I put close to your mouth the ear of my heart so that you can tell me why it is that tears are sweet to us when we are unhappy?" (p. 75); 7, 10: "And I heard, as one hears things in the heart, and there was no longer any reason at all for me to doubt" (p. 150). The concept in Augustine implies the state in which the soul is prepared to receive illumination from God. It is reminiscent of St. Paul's image of the "circumcised heart" that appears in Romans (significantly the book Augustine "took up and read" in order to complete his conversion): "For he is not a Jew, which is one outwardly; neither *is that* circumcision, which is outward in the flesh: But he *is* a Jew, which is one inwardly; and circumcision *is that* of the heart, in the spirit, *and* not in the letter; whose praise *is* not of men, but of God" (Romans 2:28–29).

9. Harold Bloom, *The Anxiety of Influence*, p. 30.

10. Centro de Investigaciones Literarias, *Interrogando*, p. 53.

11. Ibid., p. 73.

12. Chapter 5 examines this reading of Lezama as a primitive in the context of Cortázar's own work.

13. See Erich Auerbach's "Figura," in *Scenes from the Drama of European Literature: Six Essays*, pp. 11–71.

14. Santí describes Lezama's extension of the concept of intertextual reading to history, or more specifically to what I call the emblematic use of history, the search for historical images with poetic potential: "In 'Myths and Classical Weariness,' Lezama insists on the 'difficulty of historical meaning and vision,' . . . whose solution, newly formulated, is equivalent to the intertextual reading that he himself had theoretically glimpsed sixteen years before. Lezama's new formulation, therefore, will be in terms of the participation of the image in history, a connection that offers a relational, although not necessarily chronological, sense to imaginary entities" ("Lezama, Vitier, y la crítica," p. 542).

15. For a description of Martí's stay in Saragossa, see Jorge Mañach, *Martí el apóstol*, Chapter 8, pp. 60–62. For Antonio Pérez, see John Lynch, *Spain under the Habsburgs*, 1:337–345. The best source for Pérez's life is Gregorio Marañón, *Antonio Pérez (El hombre, el drama, la época)*. Lezama also speaks of the association between Martí and Pérez in *Paradiso* (Chapter 8): "Antonio Pérez, el asesino que se rebeló opinaba que sólo los grandes estómagos digerían veneno. Por cierto que a José Martí le gustaba mucho esa frase del secretario perverso. Hay que ser muy secretario y muy perverso para enamorarse de una tuerta, sobre todo cuando sabemos que ese ojo tuerto ha sido besado por Felipe II, que el diablo siga bendiciendo por los siglos de los siglos" (1:254). ("Antonio Pérez, the assassin [who rebelled], was of the opinion that only great stomachs can digest poison. [By the way,] José Martí admired the perverse secretary's phrase. One has to be very much a secretary and very perverse to fall in love with a one-eyed woman, espe-

cially when we know the missing eye has been kissed by Philip II—may the devil bless him through all eternity" [p. 181].)

16. Marañón, *Antonio Pérez*, 2:483–484.
17. José Martí, *Obras completas*, 14:263–264.
18. Cortázar, "Para llegar a Lezama Lima," pp. 42–43.
19. Lynch, *Spain under the Habsburgs*, 1:40.
20. Tzvetan Todorov, *Mikhail Bakhtin: The Dialogical Principle*, p. 12.
21. The following passage is typical of Bloom's fundamental pessimism (not coincidentally he quotes Borges elsewhere in the book) and presents a strong contrast with Lezama: "In the contemporary poems that most move me, like the *Corsons Inlet* and *Saliénces* of A. R. Ammons and the *Fragment* and *Soonest Mended* of John Ashbery, I can recognize a strength that battles against the death of poetry, yet also the exhaustions of being a latecomer" (*The Anxiety of Influence*, p. 12).
22. A reading of a remarkable episode of *Paradiso* in the next chapter will reveal how important a model Goethe is for Lezama.

5. Textual Epiphany: A Return to Bibliomancy

1. The student demonstration described in *Paradiso* is based on two autobiographical experiences, as Lezama explained to Ciro Bianchi Ross in an interview: "Actually, in my novel I combine two student demonstrations, that of September 30 [1930] and another of 1925. In 1925 I was a boy, I was fifteen, and I was interested in the student movements of Latin America . . . and I sympathized with and admired Julio Antonio Mella, who had already founded the Federation of University Students and the first Cuban Communist Party. One day Mella organized a demonstration. . . . His aim was to knock down a statue that President Zayas, who was then in power, had had erected to himself in front of the executive mansion. I was nearby, observing the events, sheltered behind a Babylonian column and from there I saw Mella who lassoed the neck of the statue with a rope and together with a group was pulling strongly to bring it down from its pedestal. In the meantime, the police arrived armed with clubs and attacked the demonstrators who ran, and Mella was left by the monument practically alone with his head broken.

"Well, that demonstration I witnessed is combined in *Paradiso* with the one of 1930 in which I did participate. Some have asked me about the identity of the leader who appears in *Paradiso* at the head of the demonstration. It's Julio Antonio Mella, even though he had already died, murdered by Machado's henchmen. Machado was a terrible man" ("Asedio a Lezama Lima," *Quimera* 30 [1983]: 37). The student leader who was killed in the September 30, 1930, demonstration was Rafael Trejo. My thanks to Enrique Pupo-Walker for bringing this valuable interview to my attention.

2. According to Eloísa Lezama Lima, her brother often referred to José Cemí as a "Wilhelm Meister habanero." See her edition of *Paradiso*, p. 16. In "La biblioteca de José Cemí," Julio Ortega sees a dialogue between Le-

zama's *Paradiso* and certain German romantic novels, Goethe's *Wilhelm Meister*, but especially Novalis's *Heinrich von Ofterdingen:* "In effect, Novalis' unfinished novel evolves as cycle of initiations through which the young apprentice poet gradually enters a reality defined by the search of absolute poetry. That ritualization of destiny is also essential to the poetic progress of José Cemí" (pp. 510–511).

3. See Johann Wolfgang von Goethe, *Wilhelm Meister's Years of Apprenticeship*, trans. H. M. Waidson. The passage occurs in Book 7, Chapter 6.

4. For a discussion of the symbolic network surrounding Foción, see Chapter 3.

5. Richard Ellmann, *James Joyce*, rev. ed. pp. 83–84.

6. Harry Levin, *James Joyce*, pp. 28–29.

7. "We perceive, therefore, that all the scholastic scaffolding cleverly erected by Stephen to support his aesthetic viewpoint only helped to support a romantic notion of poetic language as revelation and lyrical foundation of the world, and of the poet as the only one who can give an explanation of things, a meaning to life, a form to experience, a purpose to the world" (Umberto Eco, *Le poetiche di Joyce*, p. 45).

8. Stephen's "aesthetic philosophy" is expounded in Chapter 5 of *A Portrait*. See James Joyce, *A Portrait of the Artist as a Young Man*, pp. 207–216.

9. ". . . the uncertain origin of the term "epiphany" becomes very clear when we take into account the fact that Joyce had read D'Annunzio's *Il Fuoco* and was profoundly influenced by this novel. . . . Nevertheless, it seems that none of Joyce's commentators has noticed that the first part of *Il Fuoco* is entitled precisely "The Epiphany of Fire" and that there all of Stelio Effrena's aesthetic ecstasies are precisely described as epiphanies of Beauty. Now if we go and read the parts of *Portrait* that describe Stephen's epiphanies and his moments of aesthetic exaltation, we will find quite a few expressions, adjectivization, and lyrical flights that reveal their unquestionable D'Annunzian kinship. This finally confirms the decadent connotation of the Joycean notion of epiphany and its scarce Thomistic orthodoxy" (Eco, *Le poetiche di Joyce*, p. 49n.48).

10. "Joyce's second epiphany technique does quite clearly conform to Stephen's definition of lyrical art. Although *claritas* is ultimately generated by *quidditas*, we are first aware of an effect on the beholder—Stephen, or ourselves through Stephen—not of an objectively apprehensible quality in the thing revealed; if we are to penetrate through to the *quidditas*, we must try to identify ourselves with Stephen or wrest a meaning of our own from the revelation. From the standpoint of eliminating the artist's personality from his work, this particular technique was a retrogression from the method of *Dubliners*, but it did have an advantage—in Joyce's esthetic theory, an extremely important one—of realizing the three principles, *integritas, consonantia*, and *claritas*, in a single image. The next step toward impersonal creation was to modify the image so that its *quidditas* would be unmistakeable, with its radiance attached to itself rather than to a perceiving consciousness: Joyce's third epiphany technique, which explains the difference between *Stephen Hero* and *A Portrait of the Artist*" (Irene Hendry Chayes,

"Joyce's Epiphanies," in James Joyce, *A Portrait of the Artist as a Young Man: Text, Criticism, and Notes,* ed. Chester G. Anderson, pp. 362–363).

11. ". . . the epiphany becomes merely subjective, being perceived by the neurotic mind and disturbed senses of the actor or victim, rather than by the reader; the transition to the world of delirium from the ordinary world is made without warning. There is an anguished continuity between the two 'realities,' which is probably maintained by the power that language has for Stephen, for the form of his mind is such that he has adopted the habit of turning his active or outward life into inner life by means of verbal commentary or meditation which he makes to himself; since he was a child, his secret existence has proceeded in this way—in the parallelism between his words and reality which marks him out as a potential writer" (Hélène Cixous, *The Exile of James Joyce,* trans. Sally A. J. Purcell, p. 621). Cixous's description of "the form of Stephen's mind" is equally apt for Cemí.

12. "Here it is not a question of revealing the objective essence of a thing (*quidditas*), but of revealing what that thing is worth at that moment for us, and it is the value conferred on the thing at that moment that in effect *makes* the thing. The epiphany confers on the thing a value it did not have before encountering the gaze of the artist. On this score the doctrine of epiphanies and of radiance finds itself in direct opposition to the Thomistic doctrine of *claritas:* in St. Thomas a surrender to the object and its splendor, in Joyce an uprooting of the object from its normal context, its subjection to new conditions, and a bestowal of new splendor and value upon it through the grace of creative vision" (Eco, *Le poetiche di Joyce,* p. 52).

13. "An object does not reveal itself by virtue of its verifiable objective structure, but reveals itself only because it becomes an emblem of an interior moment of Stephen's.

"Why does it become an emblem? The object that achieves its epiphany has no claim to being epiphanized other than the fact that it was epiphanized. It is not only in Joyce, but before and after him, that contemporary literature offers examples of this kind, even without theorizing, and we always note that the deed never is epiphanized because it is worthy of being epiphanized, but on the contrary it appears worthy of having achieved its epiphany because it did achieve it. Appearing through casual synchronism, or through a vague reference that is not always justifiable, within an emotional context, or as its often accidental cause, the thing becomes a cipher. If in Proust certain sudden epiphanies at least have an objective motivation based on an instance of mnemonic synesthesia (the analogy between the present sensation and the past one provokes the short circuit and drags figures, sounds, and colors in its wake), in pages like Montale's *Vecchi Versi,* for example, the moth that beat against the lamp and fell on the table 'fluttering the papers' does not seem to have had any other right to surviving in memory than that of its force, the force of a deed which imposed itself and survived all others. Only after it has become gratuitously important can an epiphanic deed be charged with meaning and become a symbol" (Ibid., p. 51).

14. See Ellmann, *James Joyce,* p. 85, for dream epiphanies and examples.

15. For an example of Lezama's poetically directed "free association," see

my discussion in Chapter 2 of the poetic epiphany Cemí undergoes when he views his mother's extracted tumor.

16. Chayes notes that "in at least three instances an epiphany helps Stephen to decide on the future course of his life: the snatch of a song from the street, contrasting suddenly with the unsmiling face of the Jesuit who has been urging him to enter a novitiate; the vision of the girl wading at the shore; and the flight of the birds about the college library, symbolizing the 'fabulous artificer' after whom he is named" ("Joyce's Epiphanies," p. 362).

17. Hugh Kenner, "The *Portrait* in Perspective," in James Joyce. *A Portrait of the Artist as a Young Man: Text, Criticism, and Notes*, ed. Anderson, pp. 416–439.

18. For the Biblical as well as the classical symbolism of the garden scene, see Pierre Courcelle, *Recherches sur les Confessions de saint Augustin*.

19. "And in my misery I would exclaim: 'How long, how long this "tomorrow and tomorrow"? Why not now? Why not finish this very hour with my uncleanness?'

"So I spoke, weeping in the bitter contrition of my heart. Suddenly a voice reaches my ears from a nearby house. It is the voice of a boy or a girl (I don't know which) and in a kind of singsong the words are constantly repeated: 'Take it and read it. Take it and read it.' At once my face changed, and I began to think carefully of whether the singing of words like these came into any kind of game which children play, and I could not remember that I had ever heard anything like it before. I checked the force of my tears and rose to my feet, being quite certain that I must interpret this as a divine command to me to open the book and read the first passage which I should come upon. For I had heard this about Antony: he had happened to come in when the Gospel was being read, and as though the words read were spoken directly to himself, had received the admonition: *Go, sell all that thou hast, and give to the poor, and thou shalt have treasure in heaven, and come and follow me.* And by such an oracle he had been immediately converted to you.

"So I went eagerly back to the place where Alypius was sitting, since it was there that I had left the book of the Apostle when I rose to my feet. I snatched up the book, opened it, and read in silence the passage upon which my eyes first fell: *Not in rioting and drunkenness, not in chambering and wantonness, not in strife and envying: but put ye on the Lord Jesus Christ, and make not provision for the flesh in concupiscence.* I had no wish to read further; there was no need to. For immediately I had reached the end of this sentence it was as though my heart was filled with a light of confidence and all the shadows of my doubt were swept away.

"Before shutting the book I put my finger or some other marker in the place and told Alypius what had happened. By now my face was perfectly calm" (Augustine, *Confessions*, pp. 182–183).

20. "Sortes Homericae and Sortes Virgilianae, involve divination by opening some poem at hazard, and accepting the passage which first turns up as an answer. This practice probably arose from the esteem which poets had among the ancients, by whom they were reputed divine and inspired per-

sons. Homer's works among the Greeks had the most credit, but the trage-
dies of Euripides and other celebrated poems were occasionally used for the
same purpose. The Latins chiefly consulted Virgil, and many curious coinci-
dences were related by grave historians, between the prediction and the
event. . . . Sortes Biblicae was divination by the Bible, which the early Christians used instead of the profane poets. Nicephorus Gregoras recommended
the Psalter as the fittest book for the purpose, but Cedrenus stated that the
New Testament was more commonly used. St. Augustine denounced this
practice in temporal affairs, but declared in one of his letters that he had
recourse to it in all cases of spiritual difficulty" ("Sortilege," *Encyclopedia of
Occultism and Parapsychology*, 2d ed.). See also "P. Vergilius Maro," *Paulys
Realencyclopädie der Classichen Altertumswissenschaft*, and "Sortes Ver-
gilianae," in Hans Biedermann, *Handlexikon der Magischen Künste von
der Spätantike bis zum 19. Jahrhundert*, 2d ed.

21. The account is found in Augustine, *Confessions* 4, 3, pp. 72–73: "I
asked him why it was then that a number of true predictions were made by
astrology, and he, within the limits of his knowledge, replied that this was
due to the force of chance which was, as it were, distributed through everything in nature. Often, for instance, while turning over haphazardly the
pages of a book of poetry, one may come upon a line which is extraordinarily
appropriate to some matter which is in one's own mind, though the poet
himself had no thought of such a thing when he was writing. So, he said,
there was no reason to be surprised if a man's soul, while quite unconscious
of what was going on inside it, should be acted upon by some higher instinct
and should, by chance and not by any kind of skill, produce an answer that
would fit in well with the affairs or the doings of the inquirer."

22. "Augustine's response to this event may be interpreted as his endeav-
oring not to qualify the altogether unsolicited and 'eventful' character of
this experience with personal wilfulness. . . . Augustine evidently wishes
the book to speak, to be a word striking his eye as a voice breaks upon one's
ears, indeed as the voice in the garden is described as having suddenly inter-
rupted him" (Robert Meagher, *An Introduction to Augustine*, p. 63).

23. "Truth must appear or speak to the person. Augustine's account of his
conversion may be interpreted as an account of his being seized and held
still both by the vision and by the voice of truth. Augustine recounts numerous moments of seeing and hearing which build toward the culminating experiences of his conversion, the vision at Ostia and the voice in the garden
(cf. Conf., 8.12, 9.10). *The moment of conversion is a moment in which a
person is given to glimpse the splendor of eternity which is forever still.* As
later reflections will point out and clarify, to glimpse eternity is to gaze momentarily, not only upon God, but also upon human being as the creation of
God, *upon the what or nature of human being. And to know the what or
the nature of human being is to possess a privileged perspective upon the
who or the person of a human being, upon oneself.* It is from this privileged
perspective, grounded in the experience of conversion, that Augustine con-
fesses his lifetime, his person. His decision to bring to mind all his yester-

days and all his tomorrows is founded upon *his experience of being held still.* The presence of lifetime to mind is founded upon the experienced presence of mind to God" (ibid., p. 61; emphasis added).

24. Eco (*Le poetiche di Joyce,* pp. 53–54) describes Joyce's preoccupation with the stasis that follows full aesthetic satisfaction: "The solution that Joyce proposes in order to distinguish aesthetic experience from common experience is this: apprehension, the second activity, implies a third, 'satisfaction,' in which the perceptive process is placated and completed. Now, the aesthetic validity of the thing contemplated is measured from the intensity of this satisfaction and its duration. Here once more he approaches the Thomistic position for which the beautiful object would be that 'in cujus aspectu seu cognitione quietetur appetitus,' *and the fullness of aesthetic perception would consist in a sort of pax, of contemplative contentment. Now this pax can be easily identified with the concept of aesthetic stasis* by means of which Joyce resolves, in the *Paris Notebook,* the Aristotelian notion of catharsis" (emphasis added).

25. Augustine notes Ambrose's ability to read silently: "When he was reading, his eyes went over the pages and his heart looked into the sense, but voice and tongue were resting" (*Confessions* 6, 3, p. 114).

26. "Goethe's novel is the story of a young man who mistakes his vocation. Wilhelm's original goal is the creation of a national German theater. At the close of the novel he has renounced his life of art and, under the guidance of the mysterious Society of the Tower, is about to embark upon a journey which will lead to a life of practical service within the community of man. Because *Wilhelm Meister* was sharply attacked on moral grounds it quickly became the rallying point for a new generation of romantic poets in Germany. The novel seemed to insist on the primacy of life over social conventions, and this was a welcome breath of fresh air to young writers. But they soon realized it was a two-edged sword, for it also insisted on the primacy of life over art and struck at the heart of the romantic notion of artistic mission. This fact is unlikely to have escaped Joyce, and *A Portrait* provides, among other things, a reaffirmation of the concept of artistic vocation" (Breon Mitchell, "*A Portrait* and the *Bildungsroman* Tradition," in *Approaches to Joyce's Portrait,* ed. Thomas F. Staley and Bernard Benstock, pp. 64–65).

6. Conclusion: The Henri Rousseau of the Latin American Boom

1. See Cortázar, "Para llegar a Lezama Lima," p. 45, and Emir Rodríguez Monegal, "La nueva novela vista desde Cuba," *Revista Iberoamericana,* 41, nos. 91–93 (1975): 654.

2. Sandra Leonard, *Henri Rousseau and Max Weber,* p. 34.

3. Sarduy, "Dispersión: Falsas notas/Homenaje a Lezama," in *Escrito sobre un cuerpo,* p. 63. See my discussion of this essay in Chapter 2, above.

4. "[The cultural or historical analogies] depend totally on an imperfectly assimilated cultural baggage which consequently appears as gro-

tesque. The imperfect nature of this assimilation with its enormous *lacunae*, its errors and confusions, and the deliberately truculent exaggerations which try to compensate for the former, in the final analysis constitutes an ideal image of underdevelopment" (Rodríguez-Luis, *La literatura hispanoamericana entre compromiso y experimento*, p. 108).

5. "I refer to the errors, certain errors of Lezama that I think are not as irrelevant as it is sometimes affirmed.

"One of these errors, which is almost systematic, is the false quotation, but not as it is expressly used by Borges or Sarduy, but with the evident purpose of not being false. The introduction of famous names and the sayings and ideas that are attributed to them badly conceal the intention to connote wisdom. Intertextuality and exact or false quotations are practically routine procedures in contemporary literature, but Lezama's practice departs from that of other authors in that in most instances the quotation is supposed to seriously corroborate the content of the text in question through the authority of the foreign text, and not only to transport bricks from one place to the other in order to destroy the original and construct a new building. Many of Lezama's quotations are less false than wrong" (Horst Rogmann, "Anotaciones sobre la erudición en Lezama Lima," in *Coloquio internacional sobre la obra de José Lezama Lima*, ed. Cristina Vizcaíno, 1:78–81).

6. Quoted in Leonard, *Henri Rousseau and Max Weber*, p. 49. The exhibition took place in New York City at Alfred Stieglitz's "Little Galleries" from November 18 through December 8, 1910. All the works exhibited had been acquired by Max Weber from Rousseau. See Leonard, pp. 47–48.

7. Cortázar, "Para llegar a Lezama Lima," pp. 57–58.

8. Henri Rousseau has become almost universally known by the nickname of "le Douanier" (the customs officer). As Shattuck and other critics have pointed out, Rousseau was in fact never a customs officer, but after his military service obtained the less distinguished job of a *gabelou* (the civil servants who collected municipal duties on merchandise brought into Paris from other parts of France). In a sense, this nickname helped to perpetuate a patronizing attitude toward Rousseau by reminding everyone of his origins as a Sunday painter. Gauguin, like Rousseau, had been a Sunday painter and like him took up a full-time career as an artist only late in life, yet no one refers to Gauguin as "the Stockbroker."

9. Shattuck, *The Banquet Years*, pp. 60–61.

10. "Only an age that had begun to revise its concept of maturity could conceive of accepting the Douanier Rousseau as an artist. For, in the simplest and purest sense, Rousseau was a child. He expressed a childlike vision of the world, and his serious whimsey appeals to the child in us. Here lies the meaning of Rousseau's 'primitivism,' for the child-man lives according to a personal primitivism which cleaves to an early stage in his own development. The history of the modern movement begins with a reaffirmed innocence of all attitudes and techniques that have made the arts beautiful and instructive and adult. Rousseau, unconcernedly starting his career at the age of forty, painted himself back into the years he had lost; in that lies

his greatness and his modernism. The atavistic-prophetic monstrosity of *Ubu Roi*, a play that Jarry wrote at fifteen, and Satie's limpid piano pieces 'for tiny hands,' composed when he was over fifty, show a similar response to an earlier self. But Rousseau's entire career was devoted to creating the universe of a grown-up child" (ibid., pp. 31–32). Also see Leonard: "To the artists, dealers and critics of the period, Rousseau appeared to have the same kind of ingenuous charm that they found in African art. Probably it was not coincidental that Joseph Brummer, Rousseau's first dealer, also was involved in Congolese sculpture. Both Basler and Weber have reported that Brummer kept his two Rousseau landscapes on a shelf surrounded by primitive African figurines" (*Henri Rousseau and Max Weber*, p. 17).

   11. Quoted in Shattuck, *The Banquet Years*, p. 111. See also the catalogue for the 1985 exhibition of Rousseau's works at the Museum of Modern Art, New York, *Henri Rousseau*, p. 250.

   12. Quoted in Shattuck, *The Banquet Years*, pp. 111–112.

   13. Ibid., p. 111.

   14. For an account of Lezama's life, see Fazzolari, *Paradiso y el sistema poético*, pp. 15–28. See also Eloísa Lezama Lima's biographical notes to her edition of *Paradiso*, pp. 16–30, and to José Lezama Lima's correspondence, *Cartas (1939–1976)*, pp. 11–40.

   15. "With you, my friend Lezama, so alert, so avid, so full, it is possible to go on speaking about poetry forever, without exhaustion or weariness, even if we sometimes do not understand your abundant notions nor your gushing expression. Other tasks, poetic and less poetic, await. Finally, thank you for your presence and your attendance with me in poetry" (quoted by Fazzolari, *Paradiso y el sistema poético*, p. 17).

   16. The *Orígenes* group included poets, painters, composers, novelists, and essayists. Among them were Gastón Baquero, Eliseo Diego, Roberto Fernández Retamar, Father Angel Gaztelu, Bella García Marruz, Fina García Marruz, Lorenzo García Vega, Alfredo Lozano, Julián Orbón, Mario Parajón, Agustín Pí, Virgilio Piñera, René Portocarrero, Mariano Rodríguez, José Rodríguez Feo, Justo Rodríguez Santos, Octavio Smith, Cintio Vitier, and María Zambrano. Although not members of the group, artists such as Wifredo Lam, José Clemente Orozco, and Rufino Tamayo also contributed their work to the journal *Orígenes*. For accounts of the importance of the journal and the *Orígenes* group, see Enrico Mario Santí, "Entrevista con el grupo *Orígenes*," in *Coloquio internacional*, 2:157–189; Alessandra Riccio, "Los años de *Orígenes*," in ibid., 1:21–36; José Prats Sariol, "La revista *Orígenes*," in ibid., 1:37–58. For accounts by members of the group, see Lorenzo García Vega, *Los años de Orígenes*, and an account in novel/memoir form, Cintio Vitier, *De peña pobre*.

   17. Cabrera Infante's pastiche of Lezama entitled "Nuncupatoria de un cruzado" forms part of the section "La muerte de Trotsky referida por varios escritores cubanos, años después—o antes," a parricidal text in which the author recounts the assassination of Trotsky through pastiches of major Cuban writers: José Martí, José Lezama Lima, Virgilio Piñera, Lydia Cabrera, Lino Novás Calvo, Alejo Carpentier, and Nicolás Guillén. See Guillermo

Cabrera Infante, *Tres tristes tigres*, p. 229. As was noted in Chapter 1, there is a marked element of parricidal parody in Sarduy's appropriation and imitation of Lezama's neo-Baroque style.

18. See José Lezama Lima, *Imagen y posibilidad*, ed. Ciro Bianchi Ross. This posthumous collection of Lezama's essays was compiled by Bianchi and contains many of Lezama's enthusiastic articles about the Revolution. For a study of the role of censorship in this anthology and the relationship of Lezama to the Cuban Revolution see Enrico Mario Santí, "La invención de Lezama Lima," *Vuelta* 102 (1985): 45–49.

19. "Condemned by the censorship of the regime, removed from circulation as soon as it appeared in a few bookstores, clamored for by the best of international intellectuals, and thanks to this, reappearing fleetingly in order to silence the protests that from every point of the compass demanded its circulation, *Paradiso* was a victory for culture and liberty. But it was a bitter victory" (*Coloquio internacional*, 1 : 87).

20. "This episode did not mark, as he suggests, the beginning of a persecution that lasted until the author's death . . . Aside from the fact that when you want to censor a book, the proper course of action is not to publish it, and *Paradiso* was published in its entirety in Cuba by Ediciones Unión, its withdrawal from bookstores for three weeks was not due to 'the censorship of the regime' but to the initiative of a low-ranking official, while its reappearance in bookstores, on the other hand, was due to a decision from the highest level, in which an international 'protest' which didn't even have time to form played no part whatsoever" (*Coloquio internacional*, 1 : 99).

21. Manuel Pereira's "José Lezama Lima: Las cartas sobre la mesa" (*Coloquio internacional*, 1 : 103–122) paints a portrait of a Lezama who unambiguously supported the Revolution. While there is ample proof of Lezama's enthusiasm for the Revolution (particularly through the 1960's), Pereira fails to confront the evidence of the correspondence published by the writer's sister in which Lezama explicitly states his desire to travel abroad and the government's refusal to grant him permission. Pereira accuses Eloísa Lezama of antirevolutionary bias in her selection of the letters and dismisses the issue of the author's desire to travel (insistent in the letters of the 1970's) by remarking that Lezama had rarely traveled abroad before 1959 (p. 119). In *Cartas*, several letters mention Lezama's desire to make visits abroad and the government's refusal to grant permission. In a letter of June 1973, he writes: "Mexico's Fondo de Cultura Económica invited me and María Luisa to visit that country. But it was not possible to resolve the matter of our leaving. As you know, the publishing company Alianza Editorial has invited me to a conference in Mexico at the Institute of Latin American Culture, but everything stays up in the air . . . [Lezama's ellipsis] I suppose that some day it will gel and then we will be able to see each other. It is worthwhile to have that hope in life" (pp. 252–253). In August 1974 he writes: "The Universidad de la Aurora in Cali, Colombia, invited me to the IV Congress of the Hispanicamerican Narrative, on condition that I would give a talk or a lecture with two other writers. The tickets arrived here in

Havana, but the result was the same as always: I was not granted permission to leave. Now I receive another invitation from the Madrid Ateneo to give some lectures. I always accept, but the result is foreseeable. I am now in a moment of my life when I need to travel, to see a little of another landscape. The renown that my work has achieved abroad would allow me to do so. But Ananke, fate is there with its fixed Cyclops' eye" (p. 257). A letter of September 1, 1974, states Lezama's view of his situation very clearly: "I remain, although against my will, immobilized, since during last year and during this I have received about six invitations to travel to Spain, Mexico, Italy, Colombia, and always with the same result. I have to stay in my little house until God wishes. I am bored and tired. At times, I write a little poem and that still keeps me on my feet" (p. 259). See also pp. 261, 270.

22. Julio Cortázar, "Encuentros con Lezama Lima," in *Coloquio internacional*, 1:12–13.

23. Ibid., pp. 14–15. About this time (in a letter of January 26, 1966, to his sisters) Lezama wrote of Cortázar: "On account of the award made annually by the Casa de las Américas, Cortázar visited us and made certain declarations praising my work and affirming that *Paradiso* is an *immense poem.* We have seen each other several times. He visited me at home and is really a charming man. He really took advantage of the years he spent in Europe. He has a very modern culture and he seems to be a man who knows what will last from our time. The essay he wrote about my novel has been an extraordinary success. I am grateful to him for it because it opened the eyes of many people who don't want to see anything" (*Cartas*, pp. 188–189).

24. For a commentary of Cortázar's corrections of the text of *Paradiso* published by Era, see Santí's "Párridiso."

25. For an example of these "acrobatics" see Santí, "Entrevista con el grupo *Orígenes*," pp. 157–189. The discussion (pp. 177–183) by Cintio Vitier and Eliseo Diego of the label "transcendentalism" used by Roberto Fernández Retamar in *La poesía contemporánea en Cuba* (1954) to describe the *Orígenes* group is a sad demonstration of the need to manufacture a revisionist view of Lezama and the *Orígenes* group in Cuba. Without totally repudiating the term assigned to them years before (and rather appropriately I feel) by a man who now plays a major role in Cuba's literary bureaucracy, Vitier and Diego try to disassociate themselves from all the philosophical connotations of "transcendentalism." The climax of this unlikely marriage of Marxism-Leninism and *Orígenes* occurs when Eliseo Diego asserts: "Catholic religiosity, Catholic theology is in no way idealist because its point of departure is precisely the creation of matter. In other words, deepdown, a Catholic is as much a materialist as a Marxist-Leninist" (p. 179).

26. Julio Cortázar, *Final del juego*, pp. 67–76.

27. On Oliveira's use of "bridges" I have benefited from my discussions with Dan Smulian, who wrote a B.A. honors thesis with me on that subject at the University of Virginia in 1986 ("Sensual Tapestries and Onions: A Comparison of the Literary Theory of Julio Cortázar and Roland Barthes, and a Study of Communication Codes in *Rayuela*").

28. Cortázar, "Encuentros con Lezama Lima," p. 13.

29. Ibid.

30. Ibid., pp. 16–17.

31. The passage in which Lezama comments on Rousseau's *Promenade* [*Walking in the Forest*] occurs as part of the description of José Cemí's asthma attack and epiphanic nocturnal readings. See Chapter 5 above.

32. See my discussion of the dragon symbolism in Chapter 2 above. The other possible meaning of "la Rue du Dragon" would be "the Street of the Dragoon," a resonance of the Napoleonic wars that brought the Rosetta Stone to Paris.

33. Jorge Luis Borges has popularized this concept in his poem "El Golem." A photograph of Lezama making a sign for the Tetragrammaton with his hands exists. See *Cartas*, p. 288.

34. See Chapter 3 above for a full discussion of the symbolical exposition of Lezama's ethics in *Paradiso*.

35. Lezama, like many others, was led astray by Apollinaire's myth-making. As Shattuck explains: "Most of the lingering falsehood stems from Apollinaire. In many articles he states that Rousseau went to Mexico with troops sent by Napoleon III to support Maximilian, and that it is the memory of the 'forbidden' tropical fruits in Central America that obsessed him in his jungle paintings. Nearly every account of Rousseau's life repeats this information, but no evidence of such a trip has ever been found in public or family records. Rousseau's imagination was capable of its own voyages" (*The Banquet Years*, p. 46). Likewise, Lezama's imagination was capable of its own voyages and of attributing to others voyages that never took place. This is the case with Baudelaire's alleged trip to the American Indies. As Roger Shattuck was kind enough to point out to me, Baudelaire's destination was India, and he never got farther than Reunion.

36. Fazzolari, *Paradiso y el sistema poético*, p. 19.

37. According to Leonard, "One senses that Weber saw something of the Talmudic patriarch in Rousseau—a romantic, almost mystical image of an elder who suffers alone and perseveres in his native wisdom. Weber describes the ambience of the Rousseau studio as a "spiritual haven, a place to recuperate, to set the young, perplexed mind at peace" (*Henri Rousseau and Max Weber*, p. 21).

38. The phrase "en su mundo interpretado" ("in their interpreted world") is borrowed from Rilke's "First Elegy": "und die findigen Tiere merken es schon,/dass wir nicht sehr verlässlich zu Haus sind in der gedeuteten Welt" ("And already the knowing brutes are aware/that we don't feel very securely at home within our interpreted world") (Ranier Maria Rilke, *Duino Elegies*, trans. J. B. Leishman and Stephen Spender, p. 20).

39. Shattuck's reading of the painting also focuses on the tension caused by the juxtaposition: "*La bohémienne endormie* owes its effectiveness to the fact that the encounter is unresolved: we cannot know whether the lion will devour the gypsy or respect her dark sleep. This picture, more than the others, provides the key to the mystery of these confrontations. In an arid desert scene of night sky and brown sand meeting in a clearly drawn horizon, a lion stares at a sleeping form clothed in brilliant colors. A still-life

arrangement of mandolin and jar in the lower corner seems to hold the whole composition motionless until one suddenly notices the lion's tail, which is lashing wildly. Its savage movement creates a frightening challenge to the stillness. Robert Melville writes of this work: 'We can abstract from *The Sleeping Gypsy* a recipe for the enigma in painting: it is the situating of utterly still, imperturbably self-contained figures in a purely formal relationship which contrives nevertheless to simulate the appearance of an encounter'" (*The Banquet Years*, pp. 91–92).

40. In her discussion of a small still life that Weber acquired from Rousseau, Leonard observes: "The most striking aspect about the painting is its perspective. Each object defines a separate unit of space, each seeming to compete with the other. . . . Rousseau knew how to handle perspective conventionally, as he did with the cherries in this still life. The only element that is not in perspective in the painting is the odd arrangement of the cup and the pitcher, and it is precisely this which gives the work its drama. These small spatial epiphanies, the points at which Rousseau demonstrates his intent, are deliberate" (*Henri Rousseau and Max Weber*, pp. 28–29).

41. Carolyn Lanchner and William Rubin, "Henri Rousseau and Modernism," in Museum of Modern Art, *Henri Rousseau*, p. 42.

42. "The most singular quality of his work, however, arises from the steady light that floods his compositions and hushes them as the world can be hushed only by high noon and moonlight. The very steadfastness of his light, denying the movement of the sun and the succession of day and night, removes his paintings from time. It represents no dramatically pregnant moment of history and no fleeting instant of visual reality. Academic classicism and impressionism never affected him deeply. Steady illumination creates an expanded present which transfixes past and future in permanencies of composition and design. *The time of Rousseau's painting is the time of abstract art.* One finds the same effect in the 'primitive' compositions of Giotto, in certain Dutch interiors of the seventeenth century, in Chardin, and then not again until the new literalness of cubism" (Shattuck, *The Banquet Years*, pp. 106–107).

43. Cortázar, "Encuentros con Lezama Lima," pp. 16–17.

44. In her notes to *Study for a Family Fishing* (Plate 13) and *Family Fishing* (Plate 14), Lanchner explains that this is hardly a new discovery: "In spite of the penetrating analysis of the relationship between the sketches and their finished states made by Ingeborg Eichmann as long ago as 1938 and subsequent observations made by Daniel Catton Rich and James Johnson Sweeney in 1942, the popular conception of Rousseau as an artist who painted the way he did because he could do no other persists. A comparison of the sketch for *Family Fishing* with the finished picture convincingly supports Eichmann's observation that 'it becomes clear from the sketches that Rousseau knew the technique of impressionism but for him it was only a preparatory stage. Beyond the impression he wanted to fix the solid object in all its completeness.' It also substantiates Rich's remark that 'seeing the sketch and completed picture side by side reveals how the artist *chose* [Lanchner's italics] his method and stylization.' Sweeney adds: 'From the

outset of his career to Rousseau 'the realist' true pictorial realism always meant something beyond an attempt to transcribe literally visual experiences of the world in nature. This is clear from the departures he was accustomed to make in his final versions of landscapes from the initial impressionistic sketches painted on the ground.' . . . Eichmann concludes with the observation that 'the paintings made after the sketches . . . show nature in a final, as it were, petrified form which has been called stiff by those who have failed to realize that it is penetrated by the passionless order of eternal things'" (Museum of Modern Art, *Henri Rousseau*, pp. 128–129).

45. Saúl Yurkievich, "La risueña obscuridad o los emblemas emigrantes," in *Coloquio internacional*, 1 : 187–208.

Works Cited

Aeschylus. *Aeschylus 1: Oresteia.* Translated by Richmond Lattimore. Chicago: University of Chicago Press, 1953.

Alonso, J. M. "A Sentimental Realism." *Review* 12 (Fall 1974): 46–47.

Arnold, Edward V. *Roman Stoicism.* 1911. Reprint, New York: Arno Press, 1971.

Auerbach, Erich. "Figura." In *Scenes from the Drama of European Literature: Six Essays,* pp. 11–71. Gloucester, Mass.: Peter Smith, 1973.

Augustine, Saint. *The Confessions of St. Augustine.* Translated by Rex Warner. New York: Mentor, 1963.

Bakhtin, Mikhail. *Problems of Dostoevsky's Poetics.* Edited and translated by Caryl Emerson. Minneapolis: University of Minnesota Press, 1984.

Barth, John. "The Literature of Exhaustion." *Atlantic Monthly* 220 (August 1967): 29–34. Also in *The Friday Book: Essays and Other Nonfiction,* pp. 62–76. New York: Putnam's, 1984.

Bataille, Georges. "La Notion de dépense." In *Oeuvres complètes,* 1: 302–320. Paris: Gallimard, 1970.

Biedermann, Hans. *Handlexikon der Magischen Künste von der Spätantike bis zum 19. Jahrhundert.* 2d ed. Graz: Akademische Druck, 1973.

Bloom, Harold. *The Anxiety of Influence.* New York: Oxford University Press, 1973.

Borges, Jorge Luis. *Obra poética.* Madrid: Alianza, 1972.

Brehier, Emile. *Chrysippe et l'ancien Stoïcisme.* Paris: Gordon and Breach, 1971.

Cabrera Infante, Guillermo. *Tres tristes tigres.* Barcelona: Seix Barral, 1983.

Centro de Investigaciones Literarias de la Casa de las Américas. *Interrogando a Lezama Lima.* Barcelona: Anagrama, 1971.

Chayes, Irene Hendry. "Joyce's Epiphanies." In James Joyce, *A Portrait of the Artist as a Young Man: Text, Criticism, and Notes,* edited by Chester G. Anderson, pp. 358–370. New York: Viking, 1968.

Cixous, Hélène. *The Exile of James Joyce.* Translated by Sally A. J. Purcell. New York: David Lewis, 1972.

Cortázar, Julio. "Encuentros con Lezama Lima." In *Coloquio internacional sobre la obra de José Lezama Lima,* edited by Cristina Vizcaíno, 1: 11–18. Madrid: Fundamentos, 1984.

——. *Final del juego.* Buenos Aires: Sudamericana, 1964.

——. "Para llegar a Lezama Lima." In *La vuelta al día en ochenta mundos,* vol. 2, pp. 41–81. Mexico City: Siglo 21, 1974.

Cortázar, Mercedes. "Entering Paradise." *Review* 12 (Fall 1974): 17–19.
Coudert, Allison. *Alchemy: The Philosopher's Stone.* Boulder, Colo.: Shambhala Publications, 1980.
Courcelle, Pierre. *Recherches sur les Confessions de saint Augustin.* Paris: Bocard, 1950.
Dante Alighieri. *The Divine Comedy: I, Inferno.* Translated by John D. Sinclair. New York: Oxford University Press, 1972.
Dictionnaire de Théologie Catholique. Paris: Librairie Letouzey et Ané, 1927.
Ducrot, Oswald, and Tzvetan Todorov. *Encyclopedic Dictionary of the Sciences of Language.* Translated by Catherine Porter. Baltimore: Johns Hopkins University Press, 1979.
Eco, Umberto. *Le poetiche di Joyce.* Milan: Bompiani, 1982.
Eliot, T. S. "Tradition and the Individual Talent." In *Selected Essays,* pp. 3–11. New York: Harcourt, 1960.
Ellmann, Richard. *James Joyce.* Rev. ed. New York: Oxford University Press, 1983.
Elorduy, Eleuterio, S. J. *El estoicismo.* 2 vols. Madrid: Gredos, 1972.
Encyclopedia of Occultism and Parapsychology. 2d ed. Detroit, Mich.: Gale Research Company, 1985.
Fazzolari, Margarita Junco. *Paradiso y el sistema poético de Lezama Lima.* Buenos Aires: Fernando García Cambeiro, 1979.
García Vega, Lorenzo. *Los años de Orígenes.* Caracas: Monte Avila, 1979.
Genette, Gérard. *Figures II.* Paris: Seuil, 1969.
Gide, André. *Corydon.* In *Oeuvres Complètes,* 9:173–347. Bruges: N.R.F., 1932.
Goethe, Johann Wolfgang von. *Wilhelm Meister's Years of Apprenticeship.* Translated by H. M. Waidson. 3 vols. London: John Calder, 1977.
González Echevarría, Roberto. *Alejo Carpentier: The Pilgrim at Home.* Ithaca: Cornell University Press, 1977.
———. "El 'Monstruo de una especie y otra': *La vida es sueño,* 3, 2, p. 725." In *Calderón: Códigos, Monstruo, Icones,* edited by Javier Herrero, pp. 27–58. Montpellier: C.E.R.S., 1982.
———. *La ruta de Severo Sarduy.* Hanover, N.H.: Ediciones del Norte, 1987.
———. *Relecturas: Estudios de literatura cubana.* Caracas: Monte Avila, 1976.
Guthrie, Donald, J. A. Motyer, Alan M. Stibbs, and Donald J. Wiseman, eds. *The New Bible Commentary Revised.* Grand Rapids, Mich.: Wm. B. Eerdman, 1970.
Jerusalem Bible. Garden City, N.Y.: Doubleday, 1966.
Joyce, James. *A Portrait of the Artist as a Young Man.* New York: Viking 1967.
Kenner, Hugh. "The *Portrait* in Perspective." In James Joyce, *A Portrait of the Artist as a Young Man: Text, Criticism, and Notes,* edited by Chester G. Anderson, pp. 416–439. New York: Viking Press, 1968.
Lanchner, Carolyn, and William Rubin. "Henri Rousseau and Modernism." In Museum of Modern Art, *Henri Rousseau,* pp. 35–89. New York, 1985.

Leonard, Sandra. *Henri Rousseau and Max Weber.* New York: Richard L. Feigen & Co., 1970.

Levin, Harry. *James Joyce.* New York: New Directions, 1960.

Lezama Lima, José. "Asedio a Lezama Lima." With Ciro Bianchi Ross. *Quimera* 30 (1983): 30–46.

———. *Cartas (1939–1976).* Edited and with an introduction by Eloísa Lezama Lima. Madrid: Orígenes, 1979.

———. *Fragmentos a su imán.* Mexico City: Era, 1978.

———. *Imagen y posibilidad.* Edited by Ciro Bianchi Ross. Havana: Letras Cubanas, 1981.

———. *Obras completas.* 2 vols. Mexico City: Aguilar, 1975–1977.

———. *Oppiano Licario.* Mexico City: Era, 1977.

———. *Paradiso.* Translated by Gregory Rabassa. 1974. Austin: University of Texas Press, 1988.

———. *Paradiso.* Edited by Eloísa Lezama Lima. Madrid: Cátedra, 1980.

Lihn, Enrique. "*Paradiso*, novela y homosexualidad." *Hispamérica* 8, no. 22 (1979): 3–21.

Lynch, John. *Spain under the Habsburgs.* 2 vols. Oxford: Basil Blackwell, 1965.

Lyons, John. *Introduction to Theoretical Linguistics.* London: Cambridge University Press, 1968.

Mañach, Jorge. *Martí el apóstol.* Havana: Editora Popular de Cuba y del Caribe, n.d.

Marañón, Gregorio. *Antonio Pérez (El hombre, el drama, la época).* 6th ed. 2 vols. Madrid: Espasa-Calpe, 1958.

Martí, José. *Obras completas,* 26 vols. (La Habana: Editorial Nacional de Cuba, 1963–1966).

Meagher, Robert. *An Introduction to Augustine.* New York: New York University Press, 1978.

Mitchell, Breon. "*A Portrait* and the *Bildungsroman* Tradition." In *Approaches to Joyce's Portrait,* edited by Thomas F. Staley and Bernard Benstock, pp. 61–76. Pittsburgh: University of Pittsburgh Press, 1976.

Museum of Modern Art. *Henri Rousseau.* New York, 1985.

Ortega, Julio. "La biblioteca de José Cemí." *Revista Iberoamericana* 41, nos. 92–93 (1975): 509–521.

Paulys Realencyclopädie der Classichen Altertumswissenschaft. Stuttgart: Alfred Druckenmüller, 1958.

Pellón, Gustavo. "*Paradiso un fibroma de diecisiete libras. Hispamérica* 9, nos. 25–26 (1980): 147–151. Also in *Lezama Lima,* edited by Eugenio Suárez-Galbán, pp. 165–170. Madrid: Taurus, 1987.

———. "Severo Sarduy's Strategy of Irony: Paradigmatic Indecision in *Cobra* and *Maitreya.*" *Latin American Literary Review* 12, no. 23 (1983): 7–13.

Pereira, Manuel. "José Lezama Lima: Las cartas sobre la mesa." In *Coloquio internacional sobre la obra de José Lezama Lima,* edited by Cristina Vizcaíno, 1 : 103–122. Madrid: Fundamentos, 1984.

Pérez Firmat, Gustavo. "Descent into *Paradiso:* A Study of Heaven and Homosexuality." *Hispania* 59, no. 2 (1976): 247–257.

Prats Sariol, José. "La revista *Orígenes.*" In *Coloquio internacional sobre la obra de José Lezama Lima,* edited by Cristina Vizcaíno, 1:37–58. Madrid: Fundamentos, 1984.

Riccio, Alessandra. "Los años de *Orígenes.*" In *Coloquio internacional sobre la obra de José Lezama Lima,* edited by Cristina Vizcaíno, 1:21–36. Madrid: Fundamentos, 1984.

Rilke, Ranier Maria. *Duino Elegies.* Translated by J. B. Leishman and Stephen Spender. New York: Norton, 1965.

Ríos-Avila, Rubén. "The Origin and the Island: Lezama and Mallarmé." *Latin American Literary Review* 8, no. 16 (1980): 242–255.

Rodríguez-Luis, Julio. *La literatura hispanoamericana entre compromiso y experimento.* Madrid: Fundamentos, 1984.

Rodríguez Monegal, Emir. "La nueva novela vista desde Cuba." *Revista Iberoamericana* 41, nos. 91–93 (1975): 647–662.

———. *Narradores de esta América.* 2 vols. Buenos Aires: Alfa Argentina, 1974.

———. "*Paradiso:* Una silogística del sobresalto." *Revista Iberoamericana* 41, nos. 92–93 (1975): 523–533.

Rogmann, Horst. "Anotaciones sobre la erudición en Lezama Lima." In *Coloquio internacional sobre la obra de José Lezama Lima,* edited by Cristina Vizcaíno, 1:77–85. Madrid: Fundamentos, 1984.

Ruiz Barrionuevo, Carmen. *El "Paradiso" de Lezama Lima.* Madrid: Insula, 1980.

Santí, Enrico Mario. "Entrevista con el grupo *Orígenes.*" In *Coloquio internacional sobre la obra de José Lezama Lima,* edited by Cristina Vizcaíno, 2:157–189. Madrid: Fundamentos, 1984.

———. "La invención de Lezama Lima." *Vuelta* 102 (1985): 45–49.

———. "Lezama, Vitier y la crítica de la razón reminiscente." *Revista Iberoamericana* 41, nos. 92–93 (1975): 535–546.

———. "Párridiso." *Modern Language Notes* 94 (1979): 343–365. Also in Suárez-Galbán, ed. *Lezama Lima,* pp. 141–164, and in Ulloa, ed., *José Lezama Lima: Textos Críticos.*

Sarduy, Severo. *Escrito sobre un cuerpo.* Buenos Aires: Sudamericana, 1969.

———. *Maitreya.* Barcelona: Seix Barral, 1978.

Shattuck, Roger. *The Banquet Years.* New York: Random House, 1968.

Souza, Raymond D. *Major Cuban Novelists.* Columbia: University of Missouri Press, 1976.

———. *The Poetic Fiction of José Lezama Lima.* Columbia: University of Missouri Press, 1983.

Suárez-Galbán, Eugenio, ed. *Lezama Lima.* Madrid: Taurus, 1987.

Todorov, Tzvetan. *Mikhail Bakhtin: The Dialogical Principle.* Minneapolis: University of Minnesota Press, 1984.

Ulloa, Justo C., ed. *José Lezama Lima: Textos Críticos.* Miami: Ediciones Universal, 1979.

———. *Sobre José Lezama Lima y sus lectores: Guía y compendio bibliográfico.* Boulder, Colo.: Society of Spanish and Spanish-American Studies, 1987.

Vitier, Cintio. *De peña pobre.* Mexico City: Siglo 21, 1978.
Yurkievich, Saúl. "La risueña obscuridad o los emblemas emigrantes." In *Coloquio internacional sobre la obra de José Lezama Lima,* edited by Cristina Vizcaíno, 1:187–208. Madrid: Fundamentos, 1984.

Index

Uhde, Wilhelm, 85, 87–88, 92, 104
Ulloa, Justo C., 120n.12
Ulysses, 79
Underdevelopment, 86, 132n.4

Valéry, Paul, 34, 50
Vargas Llosa, Mario, 47, 85, 94–95, 123n.2
Verne, Jules, 62
Vigón, Ricardo, 93
Vitier, Cintio, 58, 91, 119n.11, 125n.5, 134n.16, 136n.25

Weber, Max, 85–86, 110, 132n.2,
133n.6, 134n.10, 137n.37, 138n.40
Whitman, Walt, 54
Wilhelm Meister, 72, 74, 76, 83–84, 119n.7, 127n.2, 128n.3, 132n.26

Yurkievich, Saúl, 116, 139n.45

Zambrano, María, 134n.16
Zayas, Alfredo, 127n.1
Zen Buddhism, 14, 52, 120n.3
Zosimos, 25, 122n.16